A HISTORY OF
OLD DU...
AND
OLD ST. JAMES
NORTHAMPTON

G000271503

The Collector and Local Historian

Fred Golby's early life began in Alma Street, St James. He came to live on the new
Millway Nurseries in 1947, soon after this, his interest in Local History began,
and portrayed here is part of his 50 year long collection of photographs.
Since its inauguration, some 25 years ago, he has been a member of
the Northamptonshire Industrial Archaeological Group.

With Compliments
Golby

1

Samuel Sharp

One of the earliest photographs of Duston Iron ore mines taken in 1868
showing Mr. Samuel Sharp wearing white trousers and top hat, he quarried
for Iron ore in the county. Living in Dallington Hall at the time he had the
advantage of studying the jurassic rocks at Duston and collecting valuable
information for the Geological Society in London. Due to his endeavours as
an Archaeologist he was a leading figure in founding a museum in
Northampton and placed valuable contributions of his own into it
encouraging the Lord of the Manor to direct his mineral agent to reward the
Ironstone workers to look for and hand in coins, jewellery, metals,
pottery etc from the Duston pits. Originally a large area off the Weedon Rd
was a Roman settlement. In his later years he moved to
Great Harrowden Hall where he died in 1882.

Cover photograph: (By courtesy of Northamptonshire Libraries)
Section of Old Duston Ironstone Workings in 1868.
(Figures:- Mr. Samuel Sharp and Mr. Eldret.)

£6.99

Acknowledgements

Writing my second Duston and St. James book I am indebted to the following:

Northampton Libraries and Northamptonshire Record Office for the many years of research by myself and the late Ray Lagden who began the History of Duston in the late 1930's.
Northampton Mercury for permission to copy material from their old publications.
Express Lifts
Messrs. Church & Company
British Timken for including some of their village photographs and company's history.
The following Churches for making historic records, writings and documents available –
St. Lukes Church, St. Andrews (Duston),
Duston United Reform, St. James and Doddridge United Reform.
The Duston Railway photography and writings of the late William Bailey (Canada).
Circus World Museum (America), Express Lift Company, Head Teachers, Chairman and Governors of St. James and Duston C of E Lower Schools.

I am also indebted to the following for their valuable contributions in their wide and detailed knowledge of their locality:-

Harry Law, the late Oliver Bailey, the late Fred Dove, the late Henry Downie,
John and Kathleen Favell, Mr. & Mrs. B Faulkner, Dick Coleman, Bob Whitton, Francis Brown,
the late Bailey Fossett, J Broome, Mr. Mundy, Jack Laundon, Elizabeth Bull, Jane Addison,
Mr. and Mrs. Watts, Mrs. Bennett, Mr. Beadle, Mr. North, Cecil Swann,
Winnie Butler, Tony Edmunds.

Member of Northamptonshire Industrial Archaeological Group

The Industrial Archaeology began sometime after the last war and brings together people from all walks of life. Engineers, doctors, teachers and so on, a wide ranging group, submitting reports, and photographing their findings working on a fascinating hobby, learning about history, through tangible, visible things, looking into remains of old village crafts, old stone pits, brick works, and factories, examining disused railway tracks etc. etc. documenting and surveying, before these areas of past employment are gone for ever.

Published by J. W. F. Golby

Copyright 1992

ISBN 0 9518569 1 X

Introduction
To History of Duston and St. James

This is a History of Duston and St. James. The first part of this book was written by the late Ray Lagden who was the son of Alfred Lagden, manager of the extensive Nurseries in Duston from 1888 to 1939, for many years Ray researched into the early History of the Parish before the last war, at that time accessibility to parish people then living, plans, photography, Melbourne connections, former estate agents etc. were at his disposal. All his writings have been put together and with his brother's permission make absorbing reading of the early days of the old village of Duston. I have added my history of the larger houses and their residents of former times. Also the industrial life of Old Duston:- the Iron ore extractions, New Duston with its valuable building stone pits, the very large Hopping Hill brickworks, The famous Fossetts Circus, St. James with its large boot and shoe works. The Trams, Franklins Gardens etc. The industrial Railways of Duston and St. James. It is not easy to look back over a long period of time and visualise the day to day life of ordinary working people, when each year was a question of working long hours to survive and bring up a family. The insecure tenant farmer subject to the lord of the manors demands and the iniquitous tithing eventually resulted in large immigration to Canada from Duston at the turn of the century. The old customs that still survived until the first war: the feasts, the thankfulness of a harvest, cut and reaped by hand, Candlemas, Plough Monday, The beating of the bounds (the blessing of the crops) all were part of the seasons the countryman's life and his affinity to the Church, but great changes were coming to this parish, as the town of Northampton slowly expanded into it. Men walked miles each day to work to the Shoe factories. Iron ore firms employed and created a better paid work force. After Althorpe Station was opened huge quantities of "Ryland" Duston stone was sent away for building greatly adding to the demand for this best quality of Northamptonshire sandstone.

Town Mills, powered by steam helped bring to an end the old village water mills. Many of the millers towards the latter part of the 19th century installed steam engines into their mills to supplement the water power.

F. Golby

Old Duston, New Duston 1949

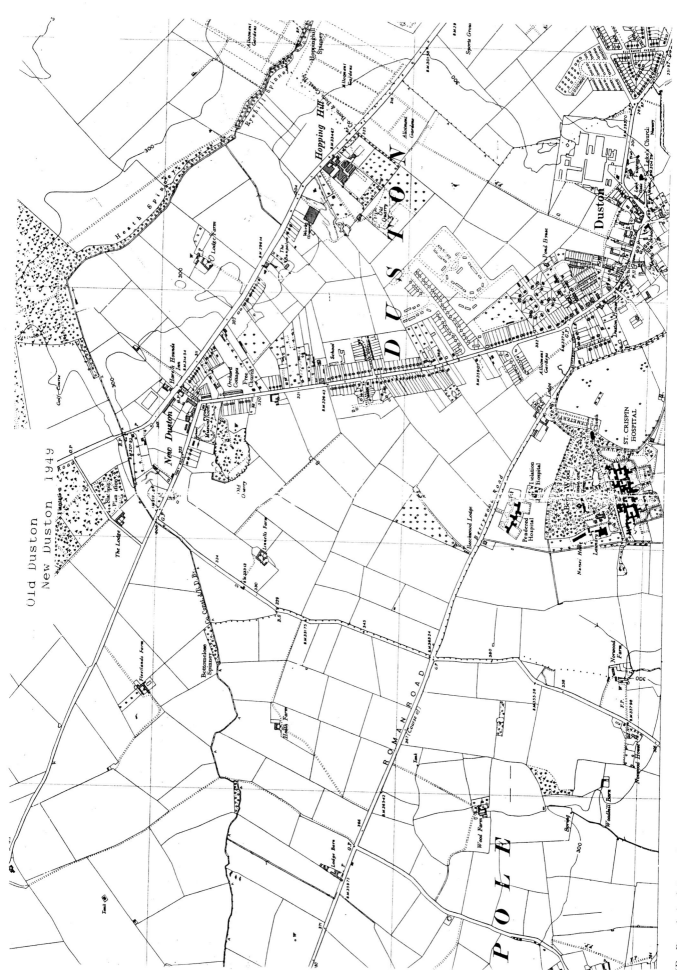

Part One – Ray Lagden's History of Duston Village

The Publisher would like to point out the following regarding Ray Lagden's history of his Duston Village & Prehistoric, Saxon, Roman and Norman Times.

Today's geologists researching into those periods of time would emerge with more updated surveys of historical evidence having at their disposal sophisticated equipment to record the past so I apologise to the reader for any discrepancy, considering these writings were made some 50 years ago and his contribution to book remains unaltered.

Prehistoric Duston

Some of the earliest information – and that of a period too remote to be assigned any definite date – we have of life in the Duston neighbourhood, points to the fact that near at hand was a sea-shore, for in the iron and stone quarries of the parish have been found samples of coral, unique star-fish, the dorsal plate of a kind of crocodile, and slabs with ripple markings, traversed in various directions by the tracks of sea-worms.

Of the Palaeolithic Age which ended about 10,000 B.C. (i.e. some 12,000 years ago, and when the natives lived in caves or huts which were often little more than wind breaks), five implements, without handles, found in the parish in 1906, are on exhibition at the Northampton Borough Museum in Guildhall Road.

In the same museum, are much more numerous exhibits from Duston, belonging to the Neolithic or New Stone Age (from 3,000 to 2,000 B.C.). By this time Palaeolithic man had long ceased his wanderings. England had probably become an island, and, in one sense, the epoch in which we now live had started. Neolithic man was probably some five feet six inches in height, with dark hair and skin much-tanned as a result of the open life he led, clad in but skins and woven flax garments. His house would (as "Historian" of the Northampton Chronicle & Echo" wrote in his "Mr. Smith" series of 1934 consist of "no more than a hut, circular in shape, built of stones piled upon one another in the same way as a country wall is made nowadays. At the height of about four feet the conical roof began. This was made of small tree trunks which sloped up from the wall to the central point. For the doorway there was a gap in the wall and a stone "porch", also roofed, was made by another wall in the shape of an "L". Entrance could only be obtained on hands and knees. The exhibits belonging to this period include worked flint flakes, chisel-shaped implements, flint scrapers, hollow scrapers for rounding arrow shafts, flint knives and flint awls or borers. All of these Neolithic exhibits from Duston came from nine arable fields on the south side of the Daventry road and to the west of the old Northampton Borough refuse tips, and are the picked specimens of 15,000 to 20,000 pieces of flint all showing the handiwork of man. Although Neolithic man invented pottery, made without a potter's wheel, none has been found in this parish.

Of the late Celtic period, which is sometimes thought to have stretched from 700 to 500 B.C. approximately, the only interesting Duston exhibit is a bronze bowl with a small hole in the bottom.

Duston in the Days of the Saxon and of the Danes

That Duston was still inhabited after the departure of the Romans we know by the fact that examples of small rough brass money, believed by experts to have been made by Romano British people, in imitation of Roman money, have been found at Duston on more than one occasion. Further, at a meeting of the Society of Antiquaries held in London on June 18th 1903 Mr. T. George (Then Librarian of Northampton) exhibited a series of bronze ornaments from Anglo-Saxon burials at Duston. At least six "unburnt" (= not cremated) burials of this period were found, and with the bodies were 8 spearheads, 7 knives and 4 shield-bosses. The ornaments of the Anglo-Saxon period found included one large square-headed brooch of bronze, one large saucer-brooch with star pattern, three open-work circular brooches and two necklaces, one of which consisted of 17 amber heads. These are now housed in the Guildhall Road Museum, Northampton as are also part of a bridle bit, an iron knife and two buckets belonging to the period and found at Duston. Indeed in an article in the Northamptonshire Natural History and Field Club Journal of June, 1919 Mr. George says that this Duston cemetery was the richest of this age in the whole county, and indicates that the number of "finds" had increased to 59 brooches, 17 necklaces of amber glass and earthenware, 7 wrist clasps, 1 girdle-hanger, 24 spear heads, 22 knives, 12 bosses of shields and the remains of a wooden bucket with bronze bands. In his "wanderings in Anglo-Saxon Britain" Arthur Weigall tells us that "as the custom of burying jewellery etc with the dead almost certainly ceased after they had adopted Christianity, most of the things must belong to the earlier period of the Anglo-Saxon invasion" (i.e. probably somewhere between 500 and 600 A.D.). Probably as early as 630 A.D. Duston was near the centre of the Anglo-Saxon kingdom of Mercia, for by that time the great Mercian King Penda had started to create a greater Mercia around the earlier settlement in the Lichfield and Tamworth district of that name. Other great kings of Mercia and who therefore exercised their rule over the Duston settlement were Ethelbald (716-757 A.D.) and Offa (757-796 A.D.).

It is interesting to construct in our mind's eye a picture of this Duston Saxon settlement. The chief would build his wooden hall, and grouped round it would be the huts of his followers and the bowers for the womenfolk. There would be the Moot Hill or place where judgment was given, and a spring for water. The whole would be surrounded by a ditch and bank, probably with a palisade fence on top. There would almost certainly be, for the use of those who made a point of attending daily prayer, not a church, but a cross, set up and consecrated to the Lord. This cross might well have been near the site of the present Church. The open-field system of farming started at this time would be, in the main, the same as that to which the execution of the Duston Enclosure Award on February 15th 1777, dealt the death blow. It should be remembered that although the remains of Anglo-Saxon Duston are much fewer than those of Roman Duston it does not follow that the former was any less important than the latter, for the Anglo-Saxon coinage was poorer and scantier than the Roman, and the implements were ephemeral.

Commencing about the year 787 the Vikings or Danes began to come to the shores of England, and after much fighting they settled in the Daneland, i.e. the land East of Watling Street. This means that Duston was just within the Danish territory, and in fact Northampton became one of their chief centres. By 910 these Danish settlers were at war with Edward the Elder, the successor to Alfred the Great, but gradually all Danes submitted to King Edward, and by 924 all England was in his hands, and the two races- the Anglo-Saxons and the Danes began to fraternise. This happy state did not unfortunately, continue, and in the year 1010 the Danish king Sweyne, and his troops burned the little township of Northampton and practically depopulated the adjacent country. Then again in the English Chronicle of 1065 we read that in that year "Morkere's northern followers dealt with the country about Northampton as if it had been the country of an enemy. They slew men, burned corn and houses, carried off cattle, and at last led captive several hundred prisoners seemingly as slaves. The blow was so severe that it was remembered, even where one would have thought that all other lesser wrongs would have been forgotten in the general overthrow of England. Northamptonshire and the shires near it were for many winters "the worse". In Volume 1 of the Victoria County History of Northamptonshire, the opinion is expressed that in readiness for the attack on the district around Northampton, Eadwine, in coming to his brother Morkere's help, must "with his Mercian and Welsh host, have marched down the Watling Street... striking off through Whilton, Brington, Althorpe, Harlestone and passing between Dallington and Duston to join his brother at Northampton.

What a sorry place this mid-11th Century Duston must have been'

Although this Duston – Nobottle road does act as a parish boundary between Upton and Duston it is for so short a distance, that we should not be justified in seriously disputing its Roman origin, as a result of the statement made by Dr. E. E. Field O.B.E. B.Sc., F.R.G.S. in an article on pre-Roman roads in "The Library List" (July 1936) the journal of the Northamptonshire County Library, when he writes "It is now a generally accepted view that when a road follows a parish boundary it is almost certainly a pre-Roman origin."

As we near the close of this chapter on Duston in Roman times, it is worthy of note that when the Roman conquests in Britain had reached their utmost extent they were irregularly divided into six provinces. Northamptonshire being in the province of Flavia Caesariensis and its particular inhabitants, the Coritavi.

And have you, reader, stopped to think that the blood of these Roman Coritavi mixed with that of the Angles and other invading races, may still be running through the veins of some one or more Dustonians of today, and that allowing as many as three generations per century, they are only separated from their present-day descendants by some 45 generations, i.e. this Roman blood has only passed through some 45 persons in reaching the veins of old Jack and Mary across the street!

Duston in the Days of the Romans

It is now a firmly established fact that Northamptonshire was an important ironstone producing district in Roman times, probably about the third and fourth centuries A.D. but its fullest resources including those at Duston remained unknown until about the year 1850. When, therefore, in the middle of the last century there was a revival of the manufacture of Northamptonshire iron, the consequent digging of ironstone the neighbourhood of Duston led to the discovery of Roman remains.

The 6" ordnance survey map indicates that Roman remains were found in Duston as early as 1849. If this is correct, they were probably uncovered during the preliminary activities in connection with the Duston Ironore Company's works, which were officially opened on June 1st 1885, on the estate of Lady Palmerston. Consequently it would be after this latter date that the finds became more numerous. First odd Roman coins were found, then fragments of Castor pottery made at the settlement of that name, near Peterborough, and of Samian ware, examples of which are to be found in the Guildhall Road Museum, Northampton, some perfect Denarli (Roman silver coins, worth about 7¾d each) of the time of Septiums Severus, who was Roman Emperor from 193 to 211 A.D. and articles of bronze. At what period of the Roman occupation of Britain is it likely that this Duston settlement was commenced? Of the coins discovered at Duston in the seven years previous to 1894 there were examples belonging to the reign of some 43 emperors and empresses those of about the time of Septimus Severus, a man of African blood, are the earliest in perfect condition. This would seem to indicate that this Duston site was probably first occupied by the Romans just previous to that Emperor's reign (193 to 211 A.D.). But even if this is the date of the earliest Roman settlement at Duston the district was almost certainly visited by them about the year 50 A.D. for the Roman invasion of Britain commenced in 43 A.D. and by 54 A.D. they had progressed as far west as Exeter and Shrewsbury, and north to the River Humber. As coins of various emperors down to the time of Honorius, ruler of the western part of the Roman Empire in 410 A.D. appear in good condition, it seems safe to say that this district continued to be a centre of Roman population until they finally left England around the last mentioned date.

What would be the general appearance of the Roman Villa in Duston? The main feature of such a Roman settlement would be the house, a rather rambling building probably of stone, designed to take advantage of breeze and view (i.e. in the Duston case it would almost certainly face in a southerly direction) rather than to be symmetrical. The entrance would lead into a large courtyard around which on the north and part of the east and west sides would be the dining room, reception rooms, kitchen, various bathrooms, and on one side the slave's quarters, without any communication with the house except through the courtyard. There would also probably be a blacksmith's forge where the horses were shod and the necessary ironwork was wrought, as at Chedworth Villa not far from Cheltenham, Gloucestershire. Running between the rooms and the courtyard would be colonnaded walks with columns standing on low walls. The ground floor walls would probably be covered with stucco and coloured.

The question of Roman roads within our parish is not one which any conclusive evidence can be focussed. The opinion has been expressed that Port Road, New Duston had a Roman origin, and that it took its name from the Latin word "porto" (I carry), indicating its use for transport purposes in Roman times. This view is not supported by Mr. B.S. O'Neil of H.M. Office of Works, who has personally inspected the Port Way in Harlestone parish an extension of Port Road, New Duston. His view is that the old Port Roads are ancient trackway (i.e. pre-Roman). He does however, surmise that the road leading from Duston past Berrywood through Nobottle and Norton to Daventry is a Roman road, for a villa has been found on either side – one in Harpole parish and one between Lower Harlestone and Nobottle. It therefore seems likely that the old trackway (Port Road) and the Roman road have existed side by side since Roman days. Mr. O'Neil's opinion as to the Roman origin of the Duston – Nobottle – Norton – Daventry road is supported by an article published in the Journal of the Northamptonshire Natural History Society and Field Club for September 1913 in which the important Roman settlement of Bannaventa (Bennavenna or Bannaventum) is stated probably to have been near the point where the Roman Watling Street crosses the above mentioned road.

Duston in the Days of the Normans

As a result of the Norman Conquest of England which took from 1066 to 1072 to complete, the possessions of Gitda, who had been one of the leading Saxon proprietors in the County of Northampton, were transferred as a whole to William Peverel, amongst whose manors "Dustone" is founded in the Domesday Survey of 1086. Stuart A. Moore in his book on the portion of the Domesday Book relating to Northamptonshire tells us, that at the time of the Survey there were about 60 major landholders in Northamptonshire, and of these William Peverel was 35th in the list arranged in order, according to the extent of the lands of the various holders, commencing with the larger holders.

The original Latin entry in the Survey for Duston, translated reads: "The same William holds four hides in Dustone. There is land for eight ploughs. In demesne there are two ploughs and two serfs: and thirteen villeins and three bordars, with three sochmen have six ploughs. There is a mill, rendering twenty shillings and thirty acres of meadow: and eleven acres of wood. It was worth forty shillings; now it is worth a hundred shillings."

Some explanation might well be given of the various terms used in the Survey. A HIDE is generally taken to be about 120 acres. DEMESNE was simply the lord of the manor's own land. A SERF was a slave who could be disposed of at the pleasure of the lord – he could be brought or sold like cattle. A VILLEIN was part and parcel of the estate to which he belonged. He was not permitted to leave his village, sell his land or give his daughter in marriage without licence from his lord, and for which a fine was levied. The villeins were compelled to work so many days a week in the lord's demesne, and to give special service at hay time and at corn harvest in return for a holding of something like 30 acres. A BORDAR was a cottager who was granted something like 5 acres in return for service to the lord. The SOCHMAN, although free, was only just over there border line of the unfree. He was dependent on his lord and had to seek his soke or jurisdiction. A PLOUGH as mentioned in the Survey is defined in the Victoria County History as "a plough team of 8 oxen". The heavy wooden plough took a team of eight oxen to draw it, and as this was more than one man could afford one or two plough teams did the ploughing of the whole village. Other authorities do not limit the team to eight oxen. The ploughman would carry a rod 5½ yards long, sometimes called a pole or perch, with which he prodded his cattle and measured the width of the strip ploughed. When the strip was four rods wide the acre was finished.

Before we leave this Domesday Survey it is worth while to quote what the Victoria County History has to say on the matter. We shall then see exactly how the Duston account was arrived at. "In the year 1085 a Commission was sent round to attend the Hundred Courts at which each Manor was usually represented by the Priest, the Reeve and four Villeins, a sort of standing committee which represented the Manor in all business matters. On this occasion the villeins were increased to six. The questions they had to answer were: What is your Manor called? Who was lord of it in Edward the Confessor's time? How does this assessment compare with the land under cultivation? How many men are there? How many cattle? How much wood and meadow-land etc? What is it worth now in taxes and what was it worth in King Edward the Confessor's reign? These answers were translated into Latin and written down under 'Hundreds'. The final account in Domesday Book of the Manor of Duston would appear to indicate that not quite all the above questions were asked in our case – or, if they were, the answers given were unsatisfactory. The above explanatory note in the Survey shows that the first money value (40 shillings) given in the account of Duston.

Duston and Manor

The above-mentioned William Peverel, sometimes stated to be a son of William the Conqueror, founded the Abbey of St. James (Northampton), and the Priory of Lenton, near Nottingham. He died on April 27th, 1113, and was succeeded by his son William Peverel who was present at the Great Council held in the first year of the reign of King Stephen, 1136, and witnessed the laws then ratified by the king. He commanded the Nottinghamshire forces at the Battle of the Standard in Yorkshire, 1138, when the Scotch were completely defeated, but was captured with the King at the siege of Lincoln in 1141. His son, the third William Peverel, is generally understood to have forfeited most of his estates to Henry II in 1154 as a result of a charge that he had poisoned Ranulph, Earl of Chester, in 1153, and this is taken to be the case by H.O.M. Estrange (the pen-name of a well known former Dustonian) in his historical novel "Mid Rival Roses", from which quotations will be given later. Another authority, however says that there is decisive evidence that the confiscation of Peverel's property was under consideration before the Earl of Chester was poisoned, for King Henry II had given to this Earl the whole of Peverel's land, unless the latter could clear himself of the treason and wickedness with which he was charged, so that the presumption is, that the administration of poison, if the story is true, was an act of revenge on the Earl for his intended acceptance of Peverel's lands, and that the offence leading to the forfeiture was Peverel's support of King Stephen. Whatever may have been the cause, as will be seen later, in the account of the Honor of Peverel, the Peverel family were allowed to keep only a very small part of their original estate, and Duston was, in the main, given by the King to Walkelin, who became Abbot of St. James in 1180. In 1205-6 during the reign of King John of Magna Charta fame when Walkelin died his son William de Duston secured permission from the King to hold all the land in Duston which Walkelin possessed when he became a monk. This permission is set out in full in the Rotuli Cartarsin (Charter Rolls) preserved at the Public Record Office and which, translated from the Latin, reads: "John by the grace of God...... You must know that we have granted and by this our present charter have confirmed to William son of Walkelin of Duston all the land with all its appurtenances which Walkelin his father held in Duston on the day on which he took the habit of Religion to hold to the same William and his heirs.

An entry in the Calendar of Close Rolls in the year 1216 reads, when translated, as follows: "Order is given to William Aynder that he cause Roger de Nevill to have the manors of Duston and of Daylington which were of William de Duston and Geoffrey Lucy if they be worth sixty pounds and unless they be worth 60 marks let him make up that sixty pounds worth of land from Waldegrave and Wande. Witness the King at Whitchurch 8 August," Whilst another entry of 1223 would seem to indicate that the manor had then passed to John de Erleigh. Here is its message: "The King to Brian de Insula, greeting, we bid you that you cause John De Erleigh to have eight does and two stags in our forest of Blackmore or two fawns to put in his park of Duston,"

By 1296 the Manor was held by John de Grey, and in 1305 Isabella de Grey died in possession of it. She was succeeded by John de Grey, her grandson, who in his turn was followed by his son John. In 1316 this last-named John was certified to be lord of Duston and a moiety of St. James' Street. He died in 1360, and was succeeded by his son John, and the Manor continued in the de Grey family until the reign of Richard II (1377-1399), when Joan de Grey, daughter of Robert de Grey, brought it in marriage to John. Lord Deincourt of Blankney in Lincolnshire.

Here it is interesting to quote the section of the Nonac Inquisitions relating to Duston, during the time the Manor was held by the above-mentioned de Grey family. These Rolls contain the results of an inquiry taken on oath of parishioners in every parish to assess a subsidy or tax of one-ninth of certain possessions of the parish in order to meet the cost of the wars of Edward III with France. The Duston entry says: "This indenture witnesses that on the Monday next after the feast of St. Mathias the Apostle in the fifteenth year of the reign of Edward III (1341-1342) after the Conquest, Henry Athlard, John de Desborough, Thomas atte Green, William Hebern, Thomas Paluer, William Brampton, Simon Faber, John Bonetoun, John Thurkil, Thomas son of Henry, John Bruyere and William Morin sworn and charged before the abbot of St. James without Northampton and his fellow assessors and sellers of sheaves, fleeces, and lambs in the County of Northampton granted to our Lord the King, say upon their oath that the ninths of the aforesaid sheaves, fleeces and lambs in Duston according to true value in the year last past were worth six marks. And did not reach the tax of the church of the vill aforesaid which tax indeed is eleven marks and the pension of the same church brings to the Prior of Lenton twenty shillings because more commodities and profits are contained within the said tax and pension to wit two virgates of land of the dower of the church aforesaid which are worth twenty-four shillings. Item, the tithes of hay in the said year twenty shillings. Item, oblations, mortuary incomes, tithes of chickens, calves, milk, honey curtilage flax and hemp."

After the overthrow of that monarch (Richard III) by Henry Tudor (afterwards Henry VII) at Bosworth field, Leicestershire, in 1485, the possessions of Viscount Lovell, including those at Duston, were forfeited to the Crown. In 1485-6 Henry VII granted the Estate of Duston with others of Viscount Lovell, to Sir Charles Somerset, an admiral of the fleet, who in 1514, became 1st Earl of Worcester. On his death in 1526, he was succeeded by his son and heir, Henry, second Earl of Worcester and whose son, the third Earl, sold the Manor of Duston for £620 to his uncle, Sir George Somerset. In 1558-9 the estate was left by will on payment of £300, to Edward Griffin of Dingley, afterwards Attorney General, and who died in 1569. Bridges' County History contains the following description of there Manor of Duston in the seventh year of Elizabeth (i.e. 1564-1565, during the ownership of Edward Griffin): "twelve messuages, six cottages, four tofts, two dovecotes, four gardens, four orchards, three hundred acres of arable land, one hundred acres of pasture, six acres of wood, twenty acres of heath and furze, and an annual rent charge of XL (forty)s, in Duston." Baker tells us that the above Edward Griffin's son, who was probably the Edward Griffin who served as High Sheriff of Northamptonshire in 1582, transferred the Duston and other estates to Sir Christopher Hatton, the famous favourite of, and Lord Chancellor under Queen Elizabeth, and who was born at Holdenby. Support is lent to this statement by an extract culled from Mr. Tanner MS preserved at the Bodleian Library, Oxford, and dealing with the "mannours, etc...... late of Sir William Hatton, Knighte (Sir Christopher's adopted nephew and heir) deceased". The extract runs as follows: "The mannour of Duston with the appurtenances purchased by the said Sir Christopher Hatton of Ed. Griffin esquire in the xxixth yeare of her saide majesties reigne (1587-1588) which was part of the Earle of Worcester's possessions houlden of the Queenes Majesties in Chief... And are worthe by the yeare above all charges dureinge the time of the saide extent i j li (£2) but afterwards it wilbe worth yearly above all charge xxxij li vj s. viij d. (£33 6s 8d)".

If, as may be expected, the estate reverted to the normal line of descent on the death of the above Thomas Coke, its next owner would be his son. Captain John Coke, later promoted Colonel. This John Coke took a prominent part in the Revolution of 1688 which placed William II on the throne, and he died in 1692. He would be followed by his son, the Rt Hon Thos. Coke who was born on February 19th 1674, at Melbourne. Thos Coke married for his second wife. Mary Hale who was a Maid of Honour to Queen Anne, and apparently, a great favourite with the Duchess of Marlborough. He himself, was appointed to Vice Chamberlain to Queen Anne in 1711, an office he continued to hold in the reign of George I, until his death on 17th May, 1727. He it was who commenced the formation of the noted gardens at Melbourne Hall. On his death in 1727 he was followed by his son of Mary Hale, George Lewis Coke, who was born March 28th 1714 died unmarried on Jan 14th 1750-1 and was the last of the male line of the Cokes. The family estates including Duston, then came to his sister. Charlotte, who had married Matthew Lamb of Brockett Hall, Hertfordshire, and brother of Robert Lamb, Bishop of Peterborough. Later owners were Lady Charlotte Lamb's son, Peniston, born 9th January, 1748, who was created first Viscount Melbourne of Melbourne in Derbyshire on January 11th 1781, and who was created a Peer of the United Kingdom, Aug 12th, 1815. he married Elizabeth, daughter of Sir Ralph Millbank of Hannaby, Yorkshire, and was the owner of the Duston, Estate at the time of the Inclosure Award in 1777. His eldest son having predeceased him was followed by his second son, the Hon. William Lamb, 2nd Lord Melbourne, who was born at Melbourne Hall on March 15th, 1779. In 1805 on the death of his elder brother, Mr Peniston Lamb, Mr. William Lamb had abandoned the legal profession to become Whig M.P. for Leominster. On June 3rd, 1805 he married Lady Caroline Ponsonby, daughter of the Earl of Bessborough. In 1819 he was elected M.P. for the County of Hertford and when Canning took office as Prime Minister, he became Secretary for Ireland. It was on July 22nd, 1826 he succeeded to the title and estates, and became 2nd Lord Melbourne. Under Lord Grey, he accepted the office of Home Secretary. Four years later, on July 14th 1834, Lord Melbourne announced that he had been authorised to reconstruct the Ministry.

The Cowper family, A.S. Jacques in his "History of Melbourne", it is, who sets out the full titles of her grandson and successor: "Francis Thomas de Grey Cowper, seventh Earl Cowper, Viscount Fordwich in Great Britain, Baron Lucas of Crudwell, Baron Butler of Moor Park, and Baron Cowper of Wingham in England, Baron Dingwall in Scotland, Baronet and Prince of the Holy Roman Empire". He was born in June, 1834, succeeded to his father's earldom in 1856, and married, in 1870, Katharine Cecilia, eldest daughter of the fourth Marquis of Northampton.

On the return of Mr. Gladstone to power in 1880, Lord Cowper, as a prominent Whig Peer, was made Lord Lieutenant of Ireland. This was during what was, perhaps, the most troubled time in Ireland's recent history, and it was a terrible two years that Lord and Lady Cowper spent at Dublin Castle. Lord Cowper died in July, 1905, his estate being valued for probate at the immense sum of £1,179,714, of which the net personality he then severed his connections with Duston, it is interesting to recall that he was appointed, in March, 1921, "Grand Gross of the Constantine Order of St. George", by H.R.H. Comte de Caserta, for the last Englishman previously invested with the Grand Cross was King Richard I (Coeur de Lion). Lord Walker died at Melbourne Hall on May 12th, 1927, aged 87 years, his successor to Melbourne and other estates (not, of course including Duston) being his son Captain Andrew William Kerr, J.P. born 23rd March 1877. Captain Kerr died on 28th March, 1929 after serving in the Navy during World War I. His heir was Master Peter Francis Walter Kerr, born 8th September, 1922 who would, but for the 1919 sale, have been owner of the Duston Estate on the attainment of his majority. He now became Marquess of Lothian. In the ownership of his estates he (the 2nd Lord Melbourne) was succeeded by his brother, the Hon. Frederick James, third Lord Melbourne, who was born on 17th April, 1782 and died in 1853, having held the offices of Envoy Extraordinary and Minister Plenipotentiary at Vienna. In recognition of the public services rendered by the second and third Viscounts Melbourne, an imposing monument was placed in St. Paul's Cathedral.

As there was no male heir, on the death of the third Viscount in 1853, his estates came to his sister, the Hon. Lady Emily Lamb, Lady Palmerston, who was born on 21st April, 1787 had first married the fifth Earl Cowper and then, on his death, Lord Viscount Palmerston. Lady Palmerston, it was, who turned the first sod of the E. & W. Junction Railway at Towcester, on 3rd August.

The Duston estate, with others, he left to his sister, Lady Annabel Kerr, wife of Admiral of the Fleet, Lord Walter Kerr, G.C.B. (Uncle to the Marquess of Lothian), and to whom she was married in 1873. Having owned the estate for some fifteen months only she died. Oct 15th 1906, aged 60. The estate then passed to her husband, Admiral of the Fleet, Lord Walter Talbot Kerr, G.C.B. who as son of the seventh Marquess of Lothian was born on September 28th 1839 at Radley. It is interesting to recall that this former owner of the Duston estate served in the Baltic during the Crimean War, 1854-5 and with the Naval Brigade in the Indian Mutiny, where he was present at the final relief of Licknow (1858). Having joined the Navy in 1853, at the age of fourteen. Lord Walter sold the Duston Estate in July 1919, when it ceased to exist as a whole.

To return, for a moment, to Duston Hall, or Manor House, tells us that when he was writing his "History of Northamptonshire" (1822-1830), no such building remained and that when the principal manor was sold to Richard Wollaston in 1653 the specification of it included "two cottages under one roof, erected on the S. side of the site where Duston Hall stood and being on the West side of Duston Street, called the Hall Cottages, and the Hall Closes". This definitely indicates that the Hall was no longer standing at that date – four years after Charles I had walked to his execution at Westminster. Possibly the Hall had only just been demolished then, by order of Cromwell, as a further punishment to Thomas Coke, owner of the estate from 1650 to 1653, who was fined "for his delinquency to the Commonwealth". When the present house, "Hall Close" was built in 1913, in a paddock of that name, and the lawns made, the workman came across a cornice stone – thought to be the corner of one of the chimneys of the old Hall – and old stone walls. It is also interesting to note that in the Local Room of the Northampton Public Library is a pen and ink elevation, dated 1881, of a doorway of an old manor house at Duston. This may have been taken from some then existent print or drawing, but there is no proof that it refers to the Manor House or Hall. Much interesting information about the Duston Estate under its late 18th and 19th century owners is afforded by a study of a "Duston": General Report", preserved in Melbourne. Commencing with a Valuation of Duston made by Messrs. Black in 1795, when the first Lord Melbourne's estate here amounted to 1.015 acres, 2 roods, 18 poles, we read "the Hilliards (father and son) are by much the neatest and best farmers, and may be held out as examples to the rest," Of another farm, that in Bant's Lane, we read that it was "very much neglected and there is no appearance of his (the farmer's) having availed himself of the near situation to Northampton, and as there are no buildings upon it there is some doubt of all the manure from it being returned". Another extract runs as follows: "Upon comparing the Great Meadow with land of the same quality in similar situations we cannot fix less than £3 per acre, and if a term is granted tenants may be found to take a third or fourth part and join in the expense with others in finding rail fences, and even pay a greater rent than is fixed". Of the cottages on the estate it says they "are generally in a very ruinous state. As no advance is made on the rents they (the tenants) should be bound at least to keep the houses in good repair.

Messrs. Black made another "valuation" in 1805 (the year of Trafalgar), and in this we read that "a considerable part of this Estate is under a better course of management than it was in 1795 when we took our first view, but part of it being poor cold land, the improvement is not in proportion to Lord Melbourne's other estates. The mill bears no advance being short of water since the Navigation was made. To this may be added that Maule's farm (probably what we now know as "The Elms") was advanced £20 per annum in 1803 upon young Hilhard's death, and regard has been had to the buildings erected by Smith and Old Hilliard at their own expense. The cottages are now in a better state of repair than when we made our last "report". The general finance of the Duston estate in 1840 (i.e. when owned by Prime Minister Melbourne) is well shown by the following statistics:

	£	s.	d.
Rents (i.e. of farm and other land)	1762	10	6
Chief Rents (i.e. of farm and other land)		2	0
Cottage Rents (i.e. of farm and other land)	64	16	0
	£1,827	8	6

Charges

	£	s.	d.
Land Tax		14	3
Subscriptions	20	5	0
	20	19	3
Net	£1,806	9	3

By 1857 the land rents had increased to approximately £2,480 and the cottage rents to approximately £101. A note in the report for that year states that this increase was due to the fact that more land had been let "for garden" purposes and as accommodation land to Northampton. Donations (no doubt to various Duston parish funds) by the estate owner in the middle of last century were never less than £15 per annum and in 1852 amounted to as much as approximately £165.

Another mid-19th century record reads as follows: "In 1844 Mr. Loyd, the Banker, much wished to purchase this Estate, Lord Melbourne declined as it is likely to maintain it not increase its value".

A Mr. Simonds made a "valuation" of the Estate dated May 12th 1857, during the ownership of Lady Palmerston. In one place he writes. "The lands generally bear a fair appearance with the exceptions of late

Howe's occupation and a part of 'Jelly Close' (a few years ago the Duston Football Field and now partly occupied by the new Service Sales Dept. of British Timken), which are in a foul state and the necessary tillage having been neglected during the present spring gives a worse face to the land and will probably entail some loss of the rent for the current half year". Of the cottages he says, "generally in a bad state, many of them very old and dilapidated-some of them are really not fit for habitation, few have any ceiling – the bedroom being open to the thatch, some have no stairs, but a ladder in lieu. The worst of the cottages are for the most part inhabited by very old people and they would consider it a hardship to be turned out – still these ought to be either altogether removed or rebuilt". No doubt some of the worst of these cottages were those which occupied an island site at the entrance to Melbourne Lane, for these were later demolished.

In this same Report Book is a note to the effect that wheat and barley cutting in 1857 began on July 28th.

We must not infer, from the above description of Duston's cottages, that they were an exception to the rule in those days. Village cottages were almost universally in a sad state and in A.G. Street's novel "The Gentleman of the Party", which has as its background a true account of English farming life over the last 70 years, we read these words, dealing with the year 1888: "It had been many years since any landlord of a large estate had built cottages, and the tumbling down of the older ones in every village had resulted in an acute shortage. This was the chief reason for the scarcity of farm labour, since it led to so many of the young labourers seeking town employment".

Duston may therefore count itself fortunate in that it had a landlord who, in the person of Earl Cooper from 1875 to 1878 built a few up to date cottages in and near Melbourne Lane for its inhabitants.

As a close to the section of this part of our story which deals with the main Duston Estate, it is fitting to make a more detailed mention of the estate sale, held on July 3rd, 1919 at 2.30 p.m. at the Grand Hotel, Northampton. The sale catalogue tells us that the Estate was offered in 51 lots, that the solicitors for the owner, Lord Walter Kerr, were Messrs. Nicholl Manisty & Co., 1 Howard St. Strand W.C.2: the land agent, Linus O. Hubble, Esq., Estate Office, Melbourne, near Derby and the auctioneers, Messrs, Daniel Smith, Oakley and Garrard, 4-5 Charles St. St. James's Square S.W.1. The general description of the lots offered runs as follows:

"Valuable freehold, agricultural, building and accommodation land known as the Duston Estate, including the following excellent and well-watered farms known as The Elms, Homeleigh, Rose Cottage, Duston Lodge and New Duston Buildings. Also meadow land a quarry of building sandstone corn mill, allotment fields, market gardens, small holdings and cottages, together with the fully licensed free house, known as "The Melbourne Arms" the whole extending to a total area of about 1.045 acres". Amongst the more interesting detailed descriptions of individual lots may be mentioned (1) Lot 28, which is described in the catalogue as a field of accommodation arable land at the end of Duston Village, with an area of 9 acres, 1 rood, 34 poles approximately, and occupied by Mr. W. Hillson (now known as Kerrfield Estate) (2) Lot 44, which consisted of a cottage, smithy and garden in Main Road, and let to Mr. E. Perkins. (The cottage and smithy were situated on the town side of "The Chantry" and were eventually pulled down. Mr. Attwood, the smith who had worked for Mr. Perkins, becoming his own master and working in one of the farm buildings attached to the Elms Farm).

It is amusing to note the very low rentals of some of the cottages in 1919-one, in Millway, was let at £4 per annum, landlord paying rates.

The catalogue description of the water corn mill known as Duston Mill is interesting, and runs as follows: "The Corn Mill is of stone and slate and contains roller plant, shafting and overshot water wheel, gates and drawing tackle, pit wheel, 2 pairs of stones separating and scouring machine, and other fittings". At the time of the Sale the farms were much split up among various tenants. e.g. the Elms Farm of 82.784 acres had as tenants of Mr. A.E. Smith, who occupied the farm-house, Mr. W. Hillson, Messrs. Ratcliffe and Jeffery, and the Northampton Rural District Council: Rose Cottage Farm of 78.918 acres was let to Mr. W. Wilcox, who occupied the farm-house Mr. W. Hillson and the Northampton Electric Light Co. (Power House), Duston Lodge Farm of 157.575 acres, was let to Messrs, Ratliffe and Jeffery whose farm bailiff Mr. Wood lived in the house, and Mr. A.E. Smith, Holmleigh Farm of 298.147 acres, was an exception to the rule and was let in its entirety at an annual rent of £497 to Mr. C.S. Smith who occupied the farm-house.

One cannot reflect without sadness on this Estate Sale which meant not only the splitting up into divers parts of what had been, for centuries, a more or less well-ordered unity, but also the severance of a connection between Duston and the numerous illustrious owners of Melbourne Hall, Derbyshire, which had lasted in almost unbroken line since the year 1650. The Sale assuredly marked the end of Duston's unspotted village beauty.

Of the minor (less important) estates within the Parish of Duston we will briefly consider the Honor of Peverel first. When, as noted earlier, during the reign of Henry II (1154-1189) the Peverel estate was divided part was given to the King's son, John, Earl of Moreton (afterwards King John). This portion formed what was known as the Honor of Peverel. When King Richard the Lion Heart died in 1199 and John ascended the throne, the Honor of Peverel went with the crown, but in1255-6 Henry III granted the guardianship of it to William de Lisle. In 1291-2 Edward I granted the care of the Honor in the counties of Leicester, Northampton (including the Duston portion) and Buckingham to Thomas de Blaston at a yearly rent of £14 to be paid by equal portions at Michaelmas and Easter. Five years later Edward III granted it to William Bretoun of Teton for life, at £16 per annum, whilst about the year 1362 Hugh Wake obtained a grant of it. Of its later history little is known. At about the period 1820-1830 the Honor was still in the King's Lands, but the courts of the Honor of Peverel which had always been held at Duston (probably, in the early days in the body of the church, and later in the church porch) the chief manor of the Honor in Northamptonshire – were by then kept by the clerk of the peace. The jurisdiction of this Court Leet, as it was often called, seems at that date still to have extended into such widely scattered places as Duston, Harpole, Ravensthorpe with Coton and Teeton, Guilsborough, Thornby, West Haddon and Roade.

The Court Rolls of the Honor of Peverel, held at Duston for the years 1679-1739, in the possession of the Northamptonshire Record Society, contain some interesting information about Duston. The first recorded meeting of the Court for this Honor of Peverel, was held on May Day, 1679 Francis Reading, gentleman presiding. This Francis Reading would almost certainly be a member of the Reading family who presented vicars to the living of Duston in 1642, 1662 and 1663.

Almost the earliest Duston names mentioned as suitors at the Court are Samuel Stanton, Tuball Cain Lumley, Johos (john) Ask, Sarah Mutton, Johos Herne, Sarah Barnes (wid-widow) Johos Arthur (gent) Wm. Spenser.

The interesting pieces of Duston information to be gleaned from these Court Rolls include the fact that in 1734 Thomas Hillyard was sworn constable of Duston.

The Cauz, Manor was another minor or less important estate in Duston. In the year 1195 – 6 and in some following years the sheriff paid £3 13s 4d into the exchequer for the farm of Duston, the property of Roger de Cauz. This may mean that this estate was in the hands of the king until the owner came of age. In 1201 under his local name, Roger de Duston paid the king 15 marks (about £10) and a palfrey, when he took possession of all the lands which his father, Roger had held at his death. The family of Cauz appears to have died out about the year 1265, with William, the son and heir of Roger, and later owners of this estate appear to have been Reginald de Grey (about 1275) Robert de la Warde (1295) and Robert de Eton (1307). In 1350 we find that King Edward III pardoned John Garlekmongere, the younger, the transgression which he had committed by purchasing 40 acres of land, 8 acres of meadow and a yearly rent charge of 20 shillings in Duston from Nicholas, son of the above Robert de Elton, "without having first obtained the royal license". In 1355 Richard de Keselingburn (Kislingbury) gave £4 for a license to purchase certain lands and tenements in Duston from John Garlekmongere, junior. Nothing more is heard of the estate as such. It is quite likely that it was joined with the principal estate.

Further interesting points to notice in connection with the early manors or estates in the Parish of Duston are (1) that William Peverel, who founded Lenton Priory, near Nottingham, as well as St. James Abbey, gave to this Priory two "parts" of the tithe of his land in Duston, of whatever was tithable. From the Calendar of Papal Registers – Papel Letters, vol I (1198 – 1304 we find that on the 7th January, 1205 the tithes of the Prior and monks of Lenton, in Duston (and other places) were confirmed. This gift of Peverel's was given by Philip, the Prior of Lenton, to the Abbot of St. James in return for which the Abbot gave Philip a yearly sum of 20 shillings, Philip however reserving for himself one virgate of land with its tithes. In 1539 – just after the dissolution of the monasteries by Henry VIII – Nicholas Heath (Heyth) late Prior of Lenton, was found to have held an annual pension of 20 shillings yearly. In 1569 Edward Griffin who held the principal manor in Duston died possessed also of "lands late parcel of Lenton Priory". According to the Tanner MSS, preserved at the Bodleian Library, Oxford, Sir William Hatton, who was lord of the principal manor also possessed at the time of his death about the year 1596, "One close and two yard lande(s) in Duston, late parte of the monasterie of Lenton houlden of the Queenes Majestie as of her Mannour of East Greenwich worth by the yeare above all charges dueinge the time of the said extent ii li (£2) but afterwards they wilbe worth yearly above all chares xvi s (16s)". It is probable that from that date onwards this estate was handed down with the principal estate; (2) that William de Cauz who died onwards this estate was handed down with the principal estate; (2) that William de Cauz who died about the year 1265, gave 2 virgates of his estate at Duston to the Abbey of St. Mary Pratis or Delapre near Northampton. In 1545 after the dissolution of the Abbey, this land was granted to George Rithe and Thomas Grantham. It would appear, therefore, that the main divisions of the land in the parish of Duston, by about the middle of the 13th century were (1) the Principal Manor, which was increased from time to time and which was not broken up until the sale of July 3rd, 1919. (2) the Honor of Peverel: (3) the Cauz Manor: (4) the property belonging to the Abbey of St. James:

St. Luke's Church Duston

The Church of St. Luke, Duston was says an old authority, at one time dedicated to the memory of the Blessed Virgin Mary. It does not however necessarily follow that its original dedication was not in honour of St. Luke, for it is known that in the time of Henry VIII the dedication festivals were often transferred to All Saints' Day or Lady Day in order to avoid too many holidays and hence, at least for a time, the real dedication was in many cases passed over for All Saints or the Blessed Virgin Mary. It stands, possibly on the site of an earlier wooden church, on the S.E. edge of the village, almost within 100 yards of the present civil (though not the ecclesiastical) parish boundary. This however does not indicate a bad choice of position on the part of its stalwart builders of more than 700 years ago, at that time the site chosen would be near the centre of the parish, which until the beginning of the present century, extended to the West Bridge, near the Castle Station, Northampton. The church occupies a splendid position on high land which commands an extensive view of Northampton and the Nene Valley, and it is worthwhile to picture for a moment the surprise which would be registered by those early builders could they return to the scene of their labours of a bygone day and look out over the vastly different scene which Northampton now presents. One doubts whether their surprise would be mingled with pleasure!

What of the opening day? The chief visitor might well have been the Bishop of Lincoln (or his representative) for Duston was in the Diocese of Lincoln until 1541 when the Diocese of Peterborough was formed. We can picture the Lord of the Manor, the Abbot of St. James, the monks and the various officials of the Manor in the solemn procession. The whole district would be on holiday, and after the solemn rite of dedication a great feast and all kinds of games would follow.

The Church was given to the Abbey of St. James, Northampton, by William Peverel, who is reported to have been the son of William the Conqueror and who died in 1113. At first this would no doubt mean that all money given for the support of the Church passed into there hands of the Abbey, but from 1158 until 1176 Walter de Alto was permitted to serve as "Rector" of Duston on condition that he paid 5d yearly for services at the altar of St. James Abbey. In 1227 Duston became a "Vicarage" as opposed to a "Rectory", and Warine became its first known "Vicar". The change probably meant that instead of receiving all the income derived from tithes for the support of the priest in charge of the parish as had Walter de Alto and his successor as Rector, William de Northampton, Warine only received the smaller tithes, the greater corn tithe going direct to the Abbey exchequer.

Back to the exterior of the fabric of our church! The upper part of the tower is of the Decorated style of architecture and this means that, approximately, it was built between 1275 A.D. and 1375 A.D. The belfry windows each consist of two trefoiled leaded lights (i.e. their tops are divided into three sections, each section being part of a circle). The battlements, on careful observation, will be seen to have a moulding which runs along the horizontal sections, but not up the vertical ones. There are also small pinnacles at the angles of the tower. At the end of the last century the tower looked rather dilapidated with the tracery and mullion (the upright division between the two lights) out of the west belfry light, but during the incumbency of the Rev. W.C. Richardson (1897-1907) it was repointed, and the windows restored externally.

As we begin to walk round the exterior of the Church we shall notice clearly that the two windows to the East of the south porch are comparatively modern and it is generally believed that the south side of the Church was partly rebuilt between 1772-1780. We shall also observe a mass dial on the south and east walls and buttresses (mass dials are circles scratched in the stone with lines radiating from a hole in the centre. The hole held the pointer of the sundial and the radiating lines, showed certain hours at which, presumably, the various services were held. They were common 800 – 900 years ago). When we reach the north door we shall notice that it has a simple moulded arch and dripstone (to throw off the rain). The dripstone has representations of heads at each end, and there is another head over the door. The north and west fronts of the church have typical Early English (approx 1190 A.D.–1270 A.D.) buttresses or supports. The assemblage of five windows in the west wall is unusual.

Probably the most interesting feature of the exterior of the Church is the large hole in the west wall approx 5ft6" above the ground and going back some 1ft6" into the wall although no longer going right through the wall it has always been known as the "lepers squint".

The purpose of which was to allow anyone forbidden from actually entering the Church as a result of infection, illness (e.g. leprosy, black plague, all probably before Reformation Times). It is now thought there could be another explanation that they could also have been used by the Verger who could have a constant look at the vessels on the high altar without entering the Church although one wonders how many times even a hole in the wall can be moved around since its original planning some 700 years ago.

And what of the interior of the church in those long ago days? The only seating accommodation would be crude stone seats round pillars (as still to be seen at Coddington in Nottinghamshire) or stone benches round the inner walls of various parts of the church (as still exist at Cotterstock, Tansor and Warmington in

Northamptonshire). The wall "ledges" were intended for old people, especially for women and it was from the use of these that the phrase "the weakest go the wall" arose. Seats in the form of pews did not appear in the churches until the sermon became an important part of the service – seldom before the 14th century, and not until the 15th century were churches generally and systematically pewed. The floor would probably be strewn with rushes at least until the erection of the pews. There would probably be no pulpit, a piece of church furniture which was not common until the 15th century at any rate in its present fixed form. Any before that time would probably be movable ones which would be moved about at the whim of the priest. And when a fixed pulpit was the custom, it frequently had on it an hour glass in a hammered iron frame. (One was still recently to be seen at Edlesborough Church, Buckinghamshire). One likes to wonder if the glass was set in so prominent a position for the shunning of dull preachers, and the protection of their congregations. There would almost certainly be an altar at the east of the aisles, at any rate of the South aisle where the altar step still remains. Such altars would be enclosed within screens, shutting off, as a rule, the eastern part of the aisle. By the time that the chancel and the top part of the tower had been completed the chancel would almost certainly be divided from the nave by a stone or wooden screen. Above the screen would be the rood ("rood" means "cross") loft which was a platform or passage, extending across the chancel, and connected with a staircase, made either in a turret or in the thickness of the wall. The rood itself the great cross bearing the figure of Our Lord with statues of St. Mary and St. John on either side, would stand upon a beam which crossed the chancel arch above the loft. The Vicar would at certain services (perhaps to read the Gospel at Mass) ascend to the top to the rood-screen, and so would the verger every night and morning for the purpose of extinguishing and re-kindling the lights burning there. We know for certain that Duston Church really had such a screen with lights burning on it for, in 1522, Richard Curtesse left "to the rode light wether schepe (sheep) and in 1528 Thomas Blome left "to the rood lyght v (5) shepe).

The altar would almost certainly be a stone one with a cross as the central carved feature of the reredos. One or two lighted candles would be placed on it for mass and at certain seasons flowers and sweet smelling herbs would be strewn upon the floor. Either in the centre of the "quire", or as a gospel desk on the north side of the altar would stand the lectern, as reading desks or lecterns in the modern sense of the word, for congregational use, were very rare until the 16th century. Certainly near the main altar – the one in the chancel – would be the piscina (still there in the case of Duston) which was a basin with a drain leading into the earth, down which the ablutions of the priest's fingers and the rinsings of the chalice were poured. Also near the altar would probably stand an image of the patron saint, and there would be images of other saints in other parts of the church with lights burning near them. We have definite proof of the existence of such statues and their accompanying lights in Duston Church.

Fairs, markets, dramatic performances, dances, ale-sellings, were all accommodated within the church's walls, but in 1268 the Papal Legate prohibited the setting up of stalls for the display and sale of merchandise inside a church. It was only stopped very slowly, however. The dramatic performances which at first were almost universal inside churches and, as previously mentioned, at a later date in the porch, were strictly religious in origin and were meant to convey the Bible story to illiterate worshippers by enacting selected scenes. At first the actors were all in clerical orders, but later choir boys and laymen took part, with the result that gradually the interpretation of the Scriptural story became very highly exaggerated. Stages were erected and costumes were provided. (Imagine carefully this scene in the almost empty nave of Duston!)

The good characters wore white and the bad black. Heaven was represented by the top part of a three level stage, and the earth was the centre one. Consequently when the characters in black were pitched on to the floor level at the back there was no mistaking the fact that they had gone to the nether regions.

"Church ales" were common and popular, and survived well into the 19th century in some churches though probably not as recently as that at Duston. (No mention has been found of them in church registers still existing). Some time in advance of Easter or Whitsuntide, or of the anniversary day of the saint to whom the church was dedicated, the churchwardens brewed strong ale from malt supplied by the parishioners. This ale was sold in the church and on the day appointed for the sale, crowds of inhabitants and visiting relatives and friends would assemble. Booths were erected in the churchyard, bands played and games – some definitely brutal – would be indulged in. It was a regular "high day and holiday". The "church ale" was indeed a church fair – the ancestor so to speak, of the modern church bazaar or garden party. For centuries it contributed appreciable sums for church expenses and who can be surprised therefore to know that some parishes under various pretexts managed to run two, three or even four "Church ales" each year?

The church, in addition, quite likely housed a plough for use on Plough Monday after Epiphany, so that it could be blessed in the work which it was to do in ploughing ready for the sowing of seed. The church also housed the long-handled fire hook, which was used to pull "burning thatch off cottage roofs which were on fire. The hook would be kept in the nave because it was a prominent place in which the villagers would be sure to find it. Such a hook was recently still to be seen hanging on the nave wall of Eaton Bray Church in Bedfordshire. There is also little or no reason to doubt that our church, like the majority of churches in England, acted as on armory after the ordinance of King Edward I compelling every parish to maintain arms and armour with a man or men according to the population, trained to use them. The church was the usual and often the only possible place of preservation.

Church Yard

The churchyard, God's Acre, has been enlarged from time to time and the most ancient gravestones are to be found on the south side. There are several dated around 1650 with the lettering still clearly to be read indicating the local presence of a stone mason who chose his stone with care and was able deeply to engrave the stone with the necessary details. No other churchyard in the neighbouring villages possesses such ancient gravestones as Duston.

Points worthy of interest in the Churchyard are (1) the old stone carved with the letters WI in the wall to the left as one enters the last mentioned extension to the churchyard: (2) the memorial stone bearing a skull and cross-bones, and placed against the same wall near the Vicarage hand-gate. It is in memory of Richard Chambers, who departed this life on October 24th 1700 aged (92) years and bears the following unusual words: "Life is uncertain Death is shure, Sin is the wound and Christ ye cure", (3) Another old stone built into the Vicarage Wall and bearing the date 6th February, 1683. (4) The Banton tombstone containing the remains of the Rev. Peake Banton, Vicar of Duston from 1863 – 1891, and of his wife and members of his family including the Rev. Herbert Rider Banton, M.A. Chaplain to the Lord Bishop of Durham. (5) The Butlin tombstone with anchor above, containing the remains of William Butlin, formerly of Duston House and of his wife and members of his family including Sir, Wm Henry Butlin who died in 1923. (6) The grave (near the Vicarage hand-gate) of Henry Harris Brown, interred as recently as August 4th 1918. Henry Harris Brown who erected Pond House, Duston, for the use of his father and mother, was one of the leading portrait painters of the 20th Century and at one time had studios in America (where he attained eminence during the First World War) and in Chelsea. (7) The tombstone near the North door of the Church which reads, "Sacred to the memory of William Abbott who died January 3rd 1869......25 years a letter carrier in London. I spend my life in wearisome labor, To come and lie beside my neighbour". (8) The well in the churchyard marked by a block of stone, and lying to the left of the main pathway as one approaches the church. As far as is known this well was last used when there was a fire at Rose Cottage more than 50 years ago.

Another record in connection with the churchyard is that a vestry meeting held on February 1st 1872, a piece of land offered by Earl Cowper, the non-resident Lord of the Manor of Duston, to enlarge the churchyard, was accepted. It included about 14 perches at the N.W. corner of the churchyard and "lately occupied by Joseph Woolley" (who kept the "Wooden Spout" Inn), and about 17 perches on the W. side of the churchyard "Lately occupied by John Roe". In other words it extended the churchyard considerably nearer though not right up to, the site of the present Lychgate. A letter dated March 7th 1872, from the Burial Acts Office, Home Official Chambers, Westminster, to the Rev. Peake Banton indicated that on the following Tuesday the new burial ground would be inspected, whilst a further letter of 25th April, 1872 approved the proposed addition (about 1 rood in area) to the burial ground.

It is interesting to read that at the Easter Monday Vestry Meeting in 1887, the same Vicar offered to forego the letting of the churchyard for sheep-grazing, so that it might be more neatly kept and the flowers and wreaths on the graves better preserved, provided that the parishioners would contribute towards the expenses of so keeping it. Unfortunately on the following Easter Monday, the Vicar had to report that this arrangement had not been very successful!

The churchyard was again extended in 1904, during the vicariate of the Rev. W.C. Richardson, this time by some 20 perches on the left-hand side as one approaches the lychgate from the church. The land was conveyed by Earl Cowper by deed dated 21st May 1903, and this deed was signed on the back by the then Bishop of Peterborough (the Rt. Rev. E. Carr. Glyn) "as consecrated ground and part of the said churchyard" on March 9th, 1904, probably the date on which the Bishop came to consecrate it. So wet had the weather been previous to the service, that it was necessary to put down boards to walk round the extension for the actual consecration. The total cost of this extension amounted to £29.8s.6d.

The last extension of the churchyard, opposite the S.Door of the church, took place in 1924, when a small piece of glebe land, formerly part of Yarde & Co's Nurseries, was added at a cost of some £30. This was during the vicariate of the Rev. W.D. Pearson, and the extension was consecrated by Dr. C.B. Bardsley, Bishop of Peterborough, on the 26th Jan 1925.

Church Music

Before the middle of the 19th Century it was the common practice, as indicated in Thomas Hardy's "under the Greenwood Tree", for the music of a church to be provided by an orchestra, the instruments including there bass-viol and the clarinet. The earliest entry – referring to music in the old Duston Churchwarden's Account Books, which still exist, is Oct, 15 (?), 1788, "Paid for 6 Basses for the Church, 5.0", and indicated th existence of such an orchestra in Duston Church more than 150 years ago. Then again in 1796 we read "March 10, To 12 new Basses, 12.0." and in 1806 "To 6 Basses for the Church, 9.0". In the 1808 accounts we find "Paid for a Tune Book, 8.0." whilst in 1809 we learn that the "Singin Master" was paid £2.10.0. Who he was, we do not know. Candles to provide light for the choir seem to have been a frequently recurring item in the church accounts. In 1809 we read "February 24th. Paid for Six Pound of Candles at the Church for Singin 6.6", and Ap.1 Paid for 2 pound of Candles, 2.1". In Dec. 1809, the "Singin Master" was paid £2.10.0 for ten weeks. In 1810 we find an entry to the effect that "James Whitting paid Mr. Cooch for the Base Viol." The Overseer's Book also contains an entry "April 16, 1811, Reed for the Base Viol £3.17.0." Other interesting entries bearing on the music of the church in the days of the orchestra and mentioned in the Churchwarden's Account Books are Jan 2nd, 1812 "Paid for stool for the Singers, 5.6", April 26, 1830 "Paid Mr. Corby for a Base and Bow for the Parrish of Duston, £4.10.0." May 13, 1830, "Paid John Spencer for a bag for the Viol 3.0." March 24, 1831, "Mr. Ager for binding two music books 6.6." Dec 6, 1844, "Bas Viol Bow 4.0", Jan 18, 1845 Paid Mrs. Birdsall for 3 tune books, £1.9.6" May 30, 1852, "Two strings to Bass Viol 1.4" and May 17 1866. "Sold the Bass Viol, 1.5.0". No further mention seems to be made for any of the old orchestral instruments, nor does there appear to be any record that the Duston orchestra played from a gallery at the W. end of the church as was the common practice. Reverting for a brief moment to the time when Duston, along with village churches in general had an orchestra of its own, it is interesting to recall the words of Arthur Bryant, who has recently lectured on more than one occasion in the Carnegie Hall, Northampton, in his "English Sage" (1840-1940) when he writes "Until the old string and brass choirs were superseded by the new fangled organs and harmoniums, the villager played as great a part in the exercise of communal worship as the parson. Standing each Sunday in the west gallery (not in that position in Duston), these rustic instrumentalists with their copper key bugles, trombones, clarinets, trumpets, flutes, fiddles, and bass viol, represented a folk tradition that was older than squire or clergy. Yet for all their tenacious clinging to old forms and rituals –" it allus has been sung an' sung it shall be" – the string choir was doomed and the conservative democracy of the English village with it". The difficulties facing a clergyman of the middle of the last century, who decided to do away with the orchestra, are admirably described by Anne Meredith in a very pleasing novel, "Curtain, Mr. Greatheart", when she says "The choir, too presented (to the new Vicar) fresh difficulties. They consisted of a number of a rusty fiddles and violins that turned up painfully during his reading of the prayers in preparation for one of the melodramatic dissenting hymns to which the parish was accustomed. Richard sat down forthwith and wrote to London, asking for an alternative hymn-book, one more in accordance with Church of England beliefs. Although he was warned the step would be unpopular, he imported the new hymn-books and on the Saturday afternoon laid them in the pews. They looked few enough, carefully spread out, for he had paid them out of his own pocket, but they were more, as it happened, than were needed. The congregation looked at them askance. When the hymn was announced a few defiantly sang to a similar number in the old book, while most of the remainder kept silence. Only a thin trickle of sound rose on the air… by hook or crook he would procure a harmonium and do away with the detestable scraping and wheezing of an amateur orchestra that drowned the prayers and distracted the attention of those present". Although no records exist of trouble in Duston at this time, no doubt the disappearance of the old orchestra caused some heart-burning among the older members of the congregation. The late Mr. Jonas Harrison who aged more than 90, died a few years ago at his home in St. James' Northampton, and who spent the early years of his married life in the old stone house opposite Duston School, remembered the old orchestra in Duston Church, and also the barrel-organ with a limited number of tunes and played by one of the Butlin family, so called in Duston past. He believed the barrel-organ fell into disuse about the time of the coming of the Rev. Peake Banton as Vicar in 1863, and stated that for a time a pitch-pipe was used to start the choir. The Rev. Peake Banton was responsible for a "restoration" of the Church, the work on which was completed in 1866 the re-opening services taking place on Thursday, the 20th September, when the preacher at 11.30 a.m. was the Rt. Rev. Francis Jeune, Lord Bishop of Peterborough. On this day, the harmonium which had been purchased for 17 guineas, was played by Mr. Biden of Northampton. This latter information is contained in a report in the "Northampton Mercury", of September 22nd, 1866. The harmonium stood in much the same place as the present organ, and was generally played by the Vicar's wife, Mrs. Banton, who faced the chancel. The boy scholars of the Sunday School sat behind her in church, and the girls near the entrance to the present vestry. Mrs. Banton, it was, who trained the choir of some 30 members. She had a powerful voice, and regularly contributed "The Kerry Dance", at the village concerts held in the Church Day School, which was much smaller in those days. Her place at the harmonium was sometimes taken by one of her two daughters, Miss Mary Banton. Interesting entries in the churchwarden's accounts of this time tell us that on 4th January, 1870 the harmonium was tuned at a cost of 2s6d and that a grant of £1 a year was made to the singers at this time. On 23rd March, 1872 music for the harmonium cost 7s1d whilst in January, 1877 2s 0d was spent on reeds for the harmonium. In December, 1822 the singers appear to have been called the "Church Choir" for the first time. The organ was installed in 1884, and on the day of the re-opening of the Church (September 24th) after extensive "restoration", was played by Mr. Brook Sampson, Mus. Bac., of Northampton.

Church Restorations at Duston

The first restoration of Duston Church took place in 1864 – 6 when the entire church was furnished with new roofs and windows throughout, all the stone work was cleaned and the pews taken down, reduced and rearranged.

The second restoration was in 1884. On this occasion new floors were laid in the body of the church, the tower piers repointed, and the chancel, through the liberality of the patron Earl Cowper, was thoroughly restored and beautified with new oak choir stalls (designed by the Vicar) and a rich and elaborate tiled floor in three platforms. At the same time a fine new organ was added with organ and vestry screens of carved oak and a new and improved system of heating with hot air introduced. It should also be mentioned that during the Revd. Banton's incumbency, a very fine east window of stained glass was erected in the church by Mr Whitworth… and another window of the same kind by the Vicar.

The above information is principally taken from a memorandum in Rev. P. Banton's handwriting on flyleaf of one of Parish Registers

(Extract from Northampton Mercury 27/3/1891)

Re above restoration, Mr E.F. Law, Architect Abington St. Northampton offering his services, quotes £155 for re-roofing nave.

Second Restoration

The whole of the chancel has been thoroughly repaired through the liberality of Earl Cowper the cost being £230.

The floor of the sanctuary has been relaid with glazed Minton tiles and that of the Chancel with unglazed tiles both being specially designed by the Venerable Archdeacon (Lord Alwyne Compton). The walls have been recoloured and the roof made to accord with the remainder of the work. A new and beautiful altar cloth and hangings have been provided and also two new oak chairs for the Chancel one of which was the gift of Dr. Bowles. A new and handsomely designed altar rail has been fixed. New oak choir stalls designed by the Vicar (Rev. P. Banton) take the place of the old stalls and the uniformity of the whole is complete. An oak panelled vestry screen the panels being filled in with cathedral glass has been erected and at some future time it is proposed to place a corresponding screen on the other side of the church. Both the pulpit and reading desk have been moved a little so as not to obstruct the view of the chancel and both have been adorned with new and handsome frontals. The stone work of the fabric has been thoroughly cleansed and repointed and the walls re-coloured with a most suitable and becoming tint. The pews have been revarnished and the appearance of the church now leaves nothing to be desired.

The only external repair was the rebuilding of the porch and this has been carried out in a manner so as to retain the original form and revealing the original form of the Gothic windows which were walled up and are now thoroughly restored and reinstated. The work, irrespective of the gift of Earl Cowper, has cost over £300 and in addition to that a new heating apparatus by Constantine of Manchester has been fixed at a further cost of £100. The architects and builders were Messrs Roberts & Son of Weedon but the repairs have been largely superintended by the Vicar (The Rev. P. Banton) himself. A grand feature in the perfecting of the church has been the placing of a new organ in the South arch of the chancel at a cost of about £300.

(Extract Northampton Daily Chronicle 24/9/1884)

Duston Church Restorations since 1873

Chancel restored & refurnished.	1884	£230	Earl Cowper	Messrs Roberts Weedon
Nave Aisles etc. New floors, piers repointed, porch rebuilt oakscreen, altering pulpit etc.	1884	£300	Private Subscription	do.
New Organ	1884	£300	do. Hanley Staffs.	Messrs J. Stringer
New heating apparatus	1883/4	£100	do.	Messrs Roberts (Constantine, Manchester)
Organ Screen	1886	£28.15s.	do.	Messrs Roberts
Stained Glass Window (see date on window)	Since 1873	£100	Gift of Friend	Heaton Butler & Bayne
Brass Eagle Lectern	1888	£50	do.	
Removing font to present position	1888	£2	Private subs.	
New Lamps Chancel	1891	£8	do.	Benetfink & Co.
Total		£1118.15s.		

The above is a correct account of the Restoration of Duston Church since 1873.

Signed Peake Banton.

1947

Nice view of Old Churchway Duston

St. Lukes neighbourhood outing to Ashby St. Legers 1973 included Rev. L. Ellis, Ray & Eva Pike, Mr. & Mrs. Golby, Marion & Stan Watts, Mrs. Wills & Mr. Wills (son)

1945

Duston Womens' Institute group in Ray Lagden's garden Old Duston

1975

Televised morning worship at St. Lukes. In the choir was Mrs. Cosford, Bernice Williams, Miss Burnapp, Mrs. Carter, Mr. Carter, Mr. Capon, Mr. Dolman, Ray Pike

1948

Canon Turner (of St. Mary Church Far Cotton) presenting the scout silver cup to Duston Scout Group. In the photo are Mr. Ron Law, John Leach, the Scrutton brothers, Mr. Hammond

1885

Bill for Boiler Fuel at Duston Church

Duston Church before its late 19th restoration when the West side was plastered over to protect the sandstone.

June 1945 victory celebrations and service at Churchway Cenotaph

12th Century Mass dials on south wall of chancel of St Lukes Church. A wooden peg was inserted to read the time in early years of the churches history.

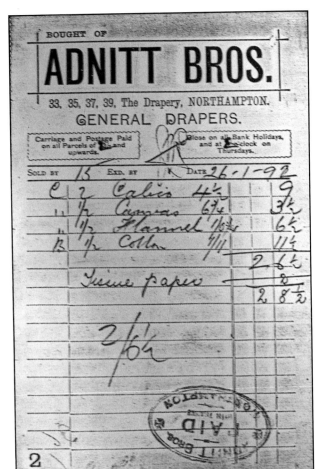

1892

Church Bill for choir vestment material

Duston Bells

The first of our bells to be cast – it had a diameter of 35 inches – was made by Robert Atton in 1619 (i.e. during the reign of James I, and some fourteen years after the gunpowder plot). Robert Atton was the son of Bartholomew Atton, and both were bell-founders at Buckingham, where Robert was buried on 6th May 1628. The second to be cast was by Henry Bagley in 1656 (i.e. during the Commonwealth – seven years after the execution of Charles I) and was 30 and a half inches in diameter, whilst the third with a diameter of 29 inches, was also made by Henry Bagley in 1670 during the reign of Charles II. The first Henry Bagley learned his craft with the Atton's at Buckingham and started his foundry at Chacombe, not far from Sulgrave, in South Northants, in 1632. His trademark was three bells, and he died in 1676. The Chacombe Foundry was carried on by his sons, Henry and William, and by his nephew, Matthew. Another Henry Bagley, the brother of Matthew, became a bell-founder at Ecton and died there in 1703. The last Bagley founder seems to have died about 1785 (i.e. four years before the French Revolution). Bagley bells are found all over the midlands, and it is of interest to note that one of the earliest complete rings of eight bells in England was cast by Henry Bagley in 1675, for St. Michael's Coventry (the now ruined Cathedral). We cannot be certain which Henry Bagley was responsible for the Duston Bells.

In the Churchwardens' (William Buther and John Phipps) Accounts for 1777 – the first year for which such accounts were still in existence – we find that two new bell ropes were purchased for 6s. 6d. Unfortunately the accounts contain no mention of the ringer or ringers. It is quite possible that there was only one, and that probably John Hall, who seems to have been the parish clerk and general church handyman at that time. We may picture, as was frequently the case in those distant days, chiming one bell with each hand the third with a foot. As we take up our story of the bells in our Parish Church we learn from the Churchwardens Accounts at the end of the 18th Century that new bell-ropes for the three bells then existing were purchased approximately every four years at a cost of some 9s. on each occasion. In 1783-84 a certain Mr. Arnold (was this the Edward Arnold of St. Neots foundry who supplied the 8 bells for St. Giles Northampton in 1783?) was paid £15 for "doing" the bells – evidently some rather extensive repairs, whilst in the Accounts for 1793-94 when W. Smith and Robt. Blewitt were the Churchwardens, we read "To Mrs. Hollowell for Ale for Thos Brooks and men mending the bell Wheels" 1s. 5d: "Paid Mrs. Claridge for ale when the bell floor was mended" 4s.2d and "To Mr. Hollowell for ale for Brooks' men, etc., "7s. 7d. Evidently the mending of the belfry floor and bell wheels was a thirst provoking job! (the Hollowells almost certainly kept the "Melbourne Arms" which was still in the control of one of that name in 1847). By 1803 the cost of a new bell-rope had risen to £1.12s.6d. In 1806 John Hilliard and Robt. Blewitt the churchwardens paid John Green 1s.6d. for "a tending and mending the bells". One naturally wonders if Green would be entrusted with the tolling of our bells on January 9th 1806, when in the midlands, bells were universally tolled for the funeral of Lord Nelson. In 1809 we find the same John Green, who almost certainly sexton at the time, was paid 8s. for ringing the bell. Daniel Tarle (Tearle) in 1814 the year before waterloo, was paid 4s. 6d: for mending the bell wheel and fastening the gudgeon (the axle) and in the same year John Green received 2s.10d. for "one day and for Oile for the bells". Charles Whiting and John Facer, Churchwardens in 1817-18, paid out £1.4s. for new bell-ropes with worsted talles (the wooden red, white and blue sallise). In the next decade one Elisha Nobles was entrusted with the mending of the bell-ropes.

To return to our Church almost opposite the Queen Victoria, Memorial Brass was the chiming apparatus (ellacombe hammers) which enabled the limited number of Hymn tunes mentioned to be played on the bells. This is rarely used before a service but the writer remembers it beginning so employed before a service of special music on the afternoon of Sunday March 24th 1935. The oak stalls under the belfry were put in during 1898 at the time of Vicar Banton, 1863-91. These dark and uncomfortable seats between the North aisle and tower were for the recognised ones at the Vicarage and the seats on the South side were for the Butlin family. Before we leave the tower let us not forget to notice the entrance, the rood loft (rood meaning cross) which was discovered and opened out during the time of Rev. Richardson 1897-1907.

The Brass Plaque

The three old bells of this church were recast, and three new bells were added by the inhabitants of the parish. W.C. Richardson, Vicar: William Jones, George Wilcox, Church wardens. Feb. 7th, 1902. The fifth bell is the original of 1656, it had its canons, or hanging loops, removed in 1901. The wording of that inscription, it is interesting to recall, was drawn up by the Rt. Rev. Lewis Clayton, the then Bishop Suffrahan of Leicester, and formerly first priest – in – charge of the church of St. James, Northampton. The memorial was the outcome of the formation of a committee consisting of the Rev. W.C. Richardson, and Messrs. G.H. Stevenson, G. Wilcox, J.V. Collier, H. Billing, W. Jones, E.S. Amos, L. West, C. Smith, W. Dove, G. Gardam, R. Bishop, J.J. Watkin, W. Blunsom, and A.R. Jones (hon.sec). The total expense of the memorial scheme was £277.11s.8d of which sum the new bells, the retuning of the old one together with the recasting of two of the latter which was cracked, and the provision of the chiming apparatus cost £258.13s.6d. The work in connection with the bells was undertaken by Messrs John Taylor & Co of Loughborough, and they were dedicated by the Bishop of Peterborough, the Rt. Rev. the Hon. E. Carr Glyn D.D. at a service held at 8.15 p.m. on Friday Feb 7th 1902.

The A & M hymn tunes which can be played on our six bells are 17, 45, 94, 109, 242, 268, 269,286, 289, 346, 393 and 415. The weights of our bells (probably only of interest to the campanologists among our readers) are Treble, 3cwts, 0 qrs, 23 lbs: 2nd, 3cwts, 1qr, 16lbs: 3rd. 3cwts, 3 qrs, 6lbs: 4th, 4 cwts, 1 qr, 3 lbs: 5th, 4 cwts, 3 qrs, 21 lbs: Tenor, 8 cwts, 0 qrs, 1 lb.

The peal is in the key of B flat and could not easily be increased in number. If extra bells were added to the present peal they would either be too small or too large for satisfactory ringing. In any case, the present bells would have to be recast first. The original inscription on the three old bells are:

1. "Henry Bagley made mee 1670"
2. "Henry Bagley made mee 1656"
3. "Robert Atton made mee 1619"

At the first recorded annual meeting of the ringers during the incumbency of the Rev. A. E. A. Jones held on January 13th, 1928, the vicar accepted office as president, and the churchwardens Mr. O. Mundy and Mr. W. Wilcox as vice-presidents. Frederick Walton was elected captain: Frank his brother, vice-captain and Henry Downie, Hon. Secretary and treasurer. At this meeting it was also decided to make all old members still resident in the parish, honorary members, namely Messrs. J. Castell, F. Cowley, W.T. Dove, H. Mallard, and A. Wilcox. Others who rang during 1928 in addition to the above mentioned officers were Messrs. R. Hopewell, C. Smith, A. Harrison and J. Taylor. In December 1929 Mr. Lloyd Wilson, who had succeeded Mr. O. Munday as churchwarden was elected a vice-president of the ringers. He in turn, was succeeded by Mr. H.L. Timpson in 1932. Other ringers during this period were Messrs. A. Harrison, C. Wright, S. Mundy, C. Handscombe, F. Paxton, and R. Cross, and by January 1933 Mr. D. Shelmerdine had joined the band, and become hon. secretary. At this same time Mr. C. Smith was elected captain and Mr. H.C. Downie vice-captain, and Tuesday evening was practice night. During 1933, Mr. Browning of Bugbrooke came over on practice nights to teach the band to ring "by method". A photograph of the ringers taken shortly before the departure of the Rev. A.E.A. Jones in July 1935, shows Mr. A.R. Jones as a vice-president, Mr. T. Bass as captain and Mr. D. Shelmerdine as vice-captain, with Messrs, H.C. Downie, J. Clifton, E. Rudkin, C. Smith and S. Munday as other members of the team which had been responsible for the ringing of a quarter peal on King George V's Jubilee Day, May 6th 1935, and on Whit-Sunday of the same year. In 1939 Taylors rehung the bells on ball bearings.

As a result of the war-time ban placed on bell-ringing by H.M. Government our bells were silent on Sunday, June 16th, 1940 and thereafter until November 15th, 1942 when church bells throughout the land rang out, to mark the 8th Army victory at El Alemein. On this day the ringers included Messrs. H. Downie, J. Taylor, F. Waltom, S. Munday, E. Nobles, C. Smith and G. Francis. Permission was again given for the bells to be rung on Christmas Day 1942 and the ban was finally lifted as the war ended.

After December 16th, 1937, the bellringers' minute book records no further meeting until March 31st, 1944, when the Rev. J.H. Butcher, whose institution and induction as Vicar of Duston had taken place on April 17th, 1943, became the new President. At this meeting Mr. S. Munday was elected Captain and Mr. H. Downie, Vice Captain, whilst the names of Mr. F. Benfield and Mr. E. Billington are included for the first time as ringers. On January 22nd, 1945 Mr. A.H. Jones became a Vice-President, in the room of Mr. A.R. Jones, whom he had previously succeeded as peoples warden. On this occasion Mr. S. Munday was re-elected Captain.

1960

Cecil Swann, Duston bell captain who has spent over 30 years teaching young people to ring here is in this team ringing for morning worship.

By courtesy of Timkin Times.

Vestry

In 1857 the total rates collected for the amount of £600. In 1859 the Vestry resolved unanimously that "any road now or hereafter to be made in the Parish of Duston and culverted to the satisfaction of the Ratepayers in Vestry would henceforth be repaired at the expense of the parish". On 11th Dec., 1862 it was decided to accept the offer of Lady Palmerston (the then owner of the Duston Estate) and others, owners of property on both sides of the road called Abbey Lane or Banbury Lane, for about 250 yards from the turnpike road, which had probably been used as a road or way since the time of St. James' Monastery, to pay half the expense of levelling and repairing the road (which was in a very bad state) and that the remainder of the expense should be defrayed by the Parish out of the Highway Rates. On March 23rd, 1863 Mr. William Wyatt Jnr. was appointed way warden under the new act, by which the old surveyor of the highway was superseded by highway boards for highway districts to which the parishes in the districts returned way wardens. At a meeting held on 15th October, 1863 it was agreed to direct a portion of the foot-path from Northampton to Harpole. On 12th Feb., 1864 Mr. G. Pell was granted permission to lay down tramways (for trucks carrying Limestone) across the road from Duston to Northampton and Dallington (the gap in the allotment wall opposite the Duston end of Bants Lane, through which the lines ran, is now filled in with a hedge). On Feb 25th, 1864, a meeting was called to consider a proposal from Mr. Collier on behalf of the inhabitants of St. James's End respecting the appointing of Parish Officers (Church-wardens, etc) It was agreed to divide the same as fairly as possible between all parts of the parish, but with the proviso that St. James's End must not choose a Dissenter as Churchwarden unless he would attend Church.

The second Vestry Books deals with the period 1865 – 1894, i.e. it goes up to the time of the formation of the Parish council. It is interesting to note that the officials present at the Vestry Meeting of March 22nd, 1866 in addition to the Vicar (The Rev. Peake Banton) were Mr. Harris (Vicar's Warden) Mr. G.F. Banton (Waywarden and NOT a relative of the Vicar) Mr. J. Smith and Mr. W. Staker (Overseers of the Poor). The entries in this second book also indicate the widespread activities of the old Vestry Meeting. At a meeting held on the 23rd August, 1866, it was carried unanimously that "the Commissioners for administering the law for the relief of the poor in England be memorialized to separate this parish from the Northampton Union" (probably in existence since 1834, or possibly even since Gilberts Act, 1782). After a further meeting to consider the requirements of the 1870 Act, it was carried that "the Vestry make application to the Education dept of the Privy Council to cause a school board to be formed for the Parish of Duston under the provision of the Elementary Education Act". At a meeting on the 23rd Feb. 1871 it was carried "that this meeting is of opinion that it is desirable and necessary to take immediate steps for removing any nuisance arising from the drainage of any part of this parish or from any other cause and with a view of improving the sanitary condition of the said Parish, a District Board should be formed under the powers of the Board of Health Act, 1848 and the Local Government Act of 1858 or any other Sanitary Act". At the same meeting it was agreed that a Committee be formed" to watch the progress of the Northampton Improvement and Extension Bill through Parliament" (There is a hint of opposition to the extension of the Borough here). On 1st February, 1872, a piece of land offered by Earl Cowper (owner of the Duston Estate, who lived at Melbourne Hall, in Derbyshire) to enlarge the Churchyard was accepted by the Vestry. On 17th May, 1872 a Vestry meeting was called for the purpose of considering the advisability of stopping up and diverting the existing public horse and carriageway (to the extent of four hundred and fifty yards) of the road to Duston from the Northampton and Weedon Turnpike Road...... and of substituting a new nearer road in lieu thereof". This was agreed to. It really means that at this meeting the first move was taken to alter the course of the Duston to Northampton Road to that which it now follows. (In actual fact the change was not finally agreed upon until 12th August, 1881). Previously, of course, the road went straight from the Duston end of Bants Lane to the Weedon Road – without any left bend which is now to be found a short distance from Bants Lane as one proceeds towards Northampton. A meeting of the Vestry was held on 30th November, 1882 at 10 a.m. (Note the hour) "To consider a plan for cleaning, restoring and heating the church and chancel". This meeting resulted in the restoration of the church which was completed in 1884. A note in connection with the Easter Monday Vestry Meeting 1885 in one of the most interesting we love, – "Some working men attended to ask if the Vestry meetings could be held in the evening as that time would be more convenient for them to attend". The Chairman, the Rev. Peake Banton, said that if the parishioners applied to him to have the vestry meeting for any given purpose in the evening he should be willing to call the meeting for the evening if the purpose of the meeting was reasonable and proper".

(The wording of the Vicars reply does not indicate that he was particularly pleased with the request). However the next meeting was held in the evening at 7 p.m. on 29th May, 1885 fill the office of overseer of the poor in the place of the late John Collier deceased. Simon Collier was appointed and his name transmitted to the magistrates. The last "Vestry meeting of the old type was held on November 8th, 1894, to elect a waywarden to serve on the Highway Board, Mr. Smalley being elected.

Parish Councils came into existence as a result of the Local Govt. Act 1894. They are now but little more than the ghosts of the old "Vestries", most of the civil powers of which are now held by the County Council or the Rural District Council. The past Duston Parish Council was elected at a Parish meeting held on 4th December 1894. A poll was demanded and on 17th December, 1894, the following Councillors were elected – Messrs Henry Billing, Wm. Smith, Edward Samuel Amos, Wm. Botterill, Harry Burt, Wm. Jones, George Alliot, Henry Trasler Harry Gough, and T.C. Thompson. The first meeting of the Council was held on 31st December, 1894 when Mr. T.C. Thompson was elected Chairman and Mr. Wm. Jones, Vice Chairman. The Assistant Overseer, Mr. W. Pynell became the first clerk.

One of the most important officers appointed by Duston "Vestries" (and indeed by "Vestries' all over the country) was the Overseer of the Poor. An Overseer's Book 1803-1819, for our own Parish is still in existence and in future "Pebbles" very interesting extracts will be given from it.

It may however, be of some interest first of all to give an outline account of the care of the poor in earlier days. Here it is:

In medieval England the care of the helpless poor was undertaken generally by the lords of the manor, the parochial clergy, the monasteries, and religious gilds, in the case of poor craftsmen by the trade gilds. In the sixteenth century the break-up of the system of the manor and craft-gild, the dissolution of the monasteries – and the increase of prices owing to the debasement of the cottage, made the question of pauperism much more pressing than it had ever been before, and some systematic attempt to provide relief was necessary to prevent social anarchy. In 1536 when Henry VIII was reigning, it was enacted that the poor who were not able to work should be provided for. For this purpose the congregation of each Parish was to be exherted to charitable offerings, and a book was to be kept by the clergy showing how the money was spent. In 1551 collections of alms at church were to be appointed, and persons refusing to subscribe were to be expostulated with the bishop; It was not however until the passage of the legislation of 1597 – 1601 that a general compulsory rating took the place of semi-voluntary contributions. The Act of 1601 (two years before the Gunpowder Plot) – was the foundation of the English Poor Law. It ordered the nomination by the justices of two or three overseers in each parish, who were empowered to raise the amount necessary for the relief of the poor by taxing every inhabitant. One act of 1662 (two years after the death of Cromwell and the accession of Charles II) authorised the justices, upon complaint of the overseers made within forty days of a person's coming to a strange parish to order him to be removed from his own place of settlement, unless he could give securities to the parish against becoming chargeable to it.

Duston Chapel – Now Duston United Reform Church

The history of Nonconformity at Duston was started by the Wesleyans as long ago as 1811 when two Northampton tradesmen named Joseph Pendrell and John Cook, trustees of Gold Street Chapel, began with 17 members.

Thirty years later they had more than doubled that number with the proud records of contributing more to the Wesleyan Circuit than any other village except Brixworth. Local Wesleyism, however, gradually faded out. The decline inspired the Baptists to fill the gap and three teachers of College Street Sunday School were pioneers in establishing a Sunday School at Duston. One was George Shrewsbury, a schoolmaster who lived in the old Welsh House at the corner of Newland and the Market Square and had an academy there. The other two were Samuel Harris, a tailor, and Robert Bartram, a draper of The Drapery. They started in the private house of the mother of Harris in Squirrel Lane at Duston. She allowed the use of her two downstairs rooms one for boys and the other for girls. In a few months, 83 scholars were enrolled and the two rooms were so overcrowded that the abandoned Wesleyan building had to be hired. Harris died three years later, leaving a daughter who married Dr. A.C. Clifton of Abington Street, and East Park Parade. His partner was Dr. Wilkinson who lived at the "Florence Nightingale" during the Crimean war. Mr. Shrewsbury who died in 1882 at the age of 84, was a native of Hackleton and it was he who discovered hidden in the cottage there that precious relic of the great Dr. Carey, the signboard that hung outside Carey's cottage when he was a shoemaker there.

Under the motherly care of College Street Church the Duston cause continued to prosper and was stimulated when as the result of Congregationalists joining the board of trustees, the name of the chapel was changed to that of the Duston Free Church and members of the Congregational churches in Northampton and district began to take an active part in helping the work.

Among them was the late Mr. C.H. Battle who died in 1952. He was invited to be hon. pastor in 1925 and was largely instrumental in the new building being added at a cost of some £4,000. He was actively as sociated with the cause for over half a century and carried out the high tradition of a most devoted body of works in the previous years. A feature of the services was the fine singing which enabled the Sunday School to win prizes at musical festivals. A special hymn was composed for them by that gifted authoress Miss Marianne Farningham Heath and was first sung at the golden jubilee celebrations in 1927. Unlike most small villages which are either in decline or with a static population Duston is ever increasing. For instance a century ago residents numbered only 714 in 1870 it had increased to 1,640.

We may well pause to ask how the (Baptist) school was run and what subjects were taught. It has been said that it was the first place in the village where the two R's (reading and writing) were taught. In minutes dated December 14th, 1828, we find that Mr. Bartram was authorised to supply "the rewards books for the Duston School". We may with some measure of safety assume that the school was run on similar lines to that at College Lane (Street) where the rules governing the way in which the school was to be conducted make quaint reading today. Under the heading of "Monitor General of Writing" is the following instruction: "To open the schoolrooms on the Sabbath morning at a ¼ before 9 o' clock. To commence the school with reading and prayer. To command "Monitors dictate" at a ¼ past 9 which command to be repeated every ¼ of an hour, allowing five minutes of that time for inspecting and sponging states and to close with singing at 10 minutes past 10 o' clock". His other duties included "To admonish and reprove when necessary......" and "to ascertain at the expiation of his monthly attendance the quantity of slates, pencils, sponges and books that are wanted and inform the succeeding Monitor general at the monthly meeting of the Committee". Another officer of the school was the "Monitor General of Reading". This officer had "to see that all the children in the school were classed according to their ability for spelling and reading to notice their progress in learning. To hear each boy repeat the scriptures that were set him on the last Sabbath. To reward them accordingly......" "Reading Teachers" and "Writing Teachers" were under the respective Monitors, and had to give such orders as "Sponge slates" or "Show slates" and also report on the children's conduct. There were rules for the children to be at school every Sunday morning at 9 o' clock "clean and decent" and in the afternoon at half past one o' clock to attend regularly, and if any child broke a slate carelessly the rule was to "procure a new one or pay", to behave with solemnity and reverence during divine worship: "to observe when public worship is over to continue orderly and quite... and then with as little noise as possible to go home moderately without loitering or playing by the way: to avoid all quarrelling and contention one with another:

to be obedient to parents, masters and teachers: on all occasions to speak the truth: and to remember to keep holy the Sabbath Day.

The publisher has been asked to add to Mr. Lagden's 1945 History of Duston, the following from the "History of Duston Chapel" by Rev. Appleton. Also the History of the Boys Brigade.

The Wesleyan cause first met in Starmers Yard (adjacent to the chapel).

The origin of the chapel began in Squirrel Lane, adult worship followed and the church was formed. 1923 a vote was taken to decide whether to form a Congregational or a Baptist Church in Duston, and in the following year 1924 by the majority vote the Congregational Church came into being.

Mr Charles Henry Battle began his long association with Duston Church in 1889 until his death in 1953. In 1925 he was invited to become lay paster and was authorised to conduct weddings there. He also held high office in various congregations including being President of the County association of 1928. His wonderful leadership at Duston led to expansion, meetings which first began in 1912 subsequently this led to adjoining property being acquired. In 1925 Mr Battle held a meeting with the Moderator of the East Midlands President of the Congregational Union regarding the Chapels future in the expanding Village. Progress continued towards larger premises by 1927 after a memorable dedication day, commemorative stones and inscribed bricks were laid. Rev A.E. Jones, Councillor Edward Lewis and the Moderator were present.

Our old and respected friend Mr. Law always pleased to tell us of his wedding at Duston Chapel in 1924 (the first held there) when Rev. Harold Bickley performed the ceremony Mrs J.D. Lewis using a gold inscribed key opened the new buildings amid great celebration. The old chapel was later renovated and electric light was installed soon after in 1928.

In 1933 a company of the girls Life Brigade was formed, under the leadership of Miss Burt and Annie Adams. Miss Burt still maintains her wonderful service to her Church.

By 1944 after meeting the Congregational Union and County association of the deacons finalised with the Moderator the needs for obtaining a Minister. The Rev. Wilkenden was invited and later inducted and this memorable service was held in October 1944.

Duston Boy's Brigade

The Boy's Brigade formed in Glasgow on October 4th 1883 by William A. Smith. First started in 1900 at Doddridge Castle Hill Congregational Church. (The 1st Northampton Company).

By 1914 Northampton had fourteen companies.

During World War 1 many officers were lost, and some companies ceased. As a result of this, in 1922 William Smith's Son, Stanley came to Northampton with a group of officers for a campaign to promote the work of the Brigade in the Town.

On the Saturday evening, Church leaders in the town were invited to attend this meeting addressed by Stanley A. Smith. Henry William Harrison, Secretary of Duston Chapel went to the Guildhall. Whilst there, he invited Stanley to preach at the Chapel on the Sunday Evening, this he did, after which Stanley spoke in the little vestry to Henry, Ames Brawn, Samuel Field, Herbert Faulkner and others about forming a Boy's Brigade in Duston. After the talks Henry said "I don't know who is going to lead it" and Stanley said "You're the man".

So on February 8th 1923 (a Thursday evening) in the Duston Congregational Free Chapel, Henry W. Harrison, 47 years and his son Arthur W. age 19 with S.H. Field started the 11th Company.

12 boys attended the first meeting, Bible Class was held each Sunday in the Chapel Gallery, and parade nights were on Thursday Evenings in the Chapel, the forms had to be removed for this.

In August, Henry, Arthur and Samuel Field took the boys (photograph available) with Northampton Battalion to camp, under canvas, to Gorleston. The officers and boys assembled at the Chapel and marched to St. Katharine's Church for the assemble, then on to the Castle Station. Shortly after the establishment of the

Company a section of the Boy's Life Brigade was formed for the younger boys.

1923-24 The Company formed a Football Team and 1924-25, A Bugle Band, (including a Drum from The Scouts which ceased in 1920).

Money was raised for a bass drum in 1928, the first bass drummer being Thomas Faulkner, the baker son, also in this year First Aid classes were started and also P.T. which Arthur was responsible for, as he was the Football and Cricket. Early success were winning the Battalion Football and Cricket Shields in 1927, and the First Aid Shield in 1928.

Although Samuel Field finished with the Brigade as an officer after two years, Henry W. Harrison and his son Arthur W. continued as Captain and Lt. serving the boys and still holds office at this present time (1950).

Sam Harrison

1927

Dedication Day. Laying the foundation stones for the new Chapel buildings in the village.

Photo of Doddridge members, thought to be taken at Doddridge Castle Hill including Philip Battle (extreme right). Lay preacher in the 1920's at Duston Chapel. A great friend of Rev. Harold Bickley.

1945

Victory celebrations outside
Duston Institute, Ashwood
Road, with Duston B.B. Band
led by Arthur Harrison,
Company Captain.

Members of Duston
Congregation Church at the
celebration of the church's
diamond jubilee 1951

Mr. Harrison's cottage
demolished 1970's to make
way for larger school
playground.

Old Duston Village

Although the Abbey of St. James will be dealt with at length later, it may be well to say something here of the Estate in Duston attached to it. In addition to the property, including the church and mill which William Peverel, the founder, gave to it, the Abbey of St. James had a considerable estate in Duston. Adelica de Weekley gave a virgate and a half (a virgate is generally taken to be about thirty acres) for the anniversary of Walkelin, her husband. Her son William de Duston, granted two virgates, with his body to be buried there. Roger de Cauz gave eight butts of land (a butt was one of the paralleled divisions of a ploughed fields contained between two parallel furrows) near the cemetery of the church of St. Mary of Duston (N.B. – St. Luke was not the patron saint of Duston Church in the first half of the thirteenth century). In 1264 William, the son of Roger de Cauz, gave Dudham (Durham?) Furlong and other lands in Duston. These were further increased at later dates. What happened to the Abbey estate in Duston at the time of the Dissolution of the Monasteries, in the reign of Henry VIII, is a debatable point, and will be dealt with later in connection with the detailed account of the Abbey.

For old-time inhabitants and for those of the younger generation who take delight in local history, the district immediately surrounding our church and vicarage is brimful of interest. In order to make a fitting approach to the tale of Church Way, the Churchyard and our Church, we therefore propose very briefly to tell the story of points of interest on the Main Road, as one approaches Church Way from Bants Lane.

Starting from that point, on the left we have glebe-land which since approximately the early nineties of last century, has been rented by Messrs. Yarde & Co, the Northampton nurserymen and florists (with the exception of the "Half Acre" almost opposite Bants Lane, which was let out as allotment. Around the year 1844, when it was, no doubt, largely rented by one of the local farmers, this land was called Church Close and across it, from the gap in the wall (now blocked by a hedge), until approximately 1888, ran a narrow-gauged railway, which went straight across the road and conveyed limestone from the pits at the back of the field opposite (First Lane End Close), to the top of the gulley in Yarde's Nursery. Here the small trucks automatically tipped their contents into other trucks waiting at the bottom of the gulley, to carry the limestone to Hunsbury Hill Furnaces, where it is believed, it was all used.

First Lane End Close (see above), in which the Factory of British Timken Ltd (the preparation of the site for which, was started on Sunday, October 12th, 1941, by a caterpillar-diesel) was originally part of the Duston Estate. In 1882 it was rented by Thos. Smalley, landlord of the "Melbourne Arms" and later by Syd Oram, his successor. On the Latter's departure for Canada, Messrs. Yarde's became tenants of the field with the exception of a small portion near Bants Lane, let to Mr. John Dunkley, on which there was a quaint little black hut known as Uncle Tom's Cabin. At the time of the Estate Sale, Messrs Yarde & Co. bought the field, and the larger portion of it remained in their possession until it was purchased by British Timken Ltd in 1941.

The original part of our present Vicarage was built in 1840-1841, during the vicariate of the Rev. Joshua Greville, who was appointed Vicar in 1811, but who for some nine years after that date, continued to act as Curate of St. George's, Hanover Square, London, leaving a (no doubt, grossly underpaid) curate in charge, who probably lived in the old vicarage at Duston. Indeed, from records investigated, it seems certain that the Rev. Greville did not reside at Duston until the new vicarage was completed. The architect was Mr. E.F. Law of Sheep Street, Northampton.

The origin of place-names is a fascinating study, and some of those within the bounds of our parish are no exception to the rule. We commence with the part of our ecclesiastical parish which borders that of St. James, Northampton, we encounter the name Abbot's Way. This quite obviously derives its title from the fact that it runs over land formerly attached to the Abbey of St. James, an Abbey for Black Canons of the order of St. Augustine founded at the beginning of the 12th century by William Peverel (Perveril) of Nottingham, who dedicated it to St. James the Apostle and allotted to it 40 acres of land, and the church and mill of Duston, towards the cost of upkeep. (When the tennis courts in front of the Express Lift Co. works were made in 1924 many old remains, doubtless of some part of the monastic estate, were found).

No Manor House is now remaining: but in the conveyance to Wollaston in 1653, the specification which is extremely minute and special, includes "two cottages under one roof, erected on the south side of the site "where Duston Hall stood, and being on the west side of Duston Street, called the Hall cottages: and the site of the said close called Hall Close. The village is about a mile and a half west of Northampton, and a short distance north of the turnpike road to Daventry. In the time of Bridges it contained "threescore houses:" By the census of 1801 there were 76 houses and 386 inhabitants: and by that of 1811, 93 houses and 408 inhabitants. The annual quota of land tax for this parish is £135.16s.9d at 4s in the £. The estimated value of real property as assessed to the property tax for the year ending April 1815 was £3071. The poor's rates for the year ending Easter 1820, amounted to £519 at 5s in the £. The feast is kept on the Sunday after St. Luke. ADVOWSON. The church and mill of Duston formed part of the original endowment of St. James Abbey by William Peverel the founder: and a second grant or ratification of them by Simon (st.Liz) Earl of Northampton, in the reign of Hen2. implies an interest acquired by him in the Peverel fee, of the existence of which this solitary fact is, I believe, the only evidence on record. The church was further confirmed to the abbey by Hugh (Wells) Bishop of Lincoln, between 1209 and 1235, and by Robert (Kilwardy) Archbishop of Canterbury, between 1272 and 1279. The rectory and advowson of the vicarage were granted, after the dissolution, to John Howe in 3 Edw. 6 (1549) Sir Augustin Nicolls died, seized of them in 1618 and was succeeded by his nephew and heir Francis Nicolls Esq afterwards created a baronet, who appears to have sold them to Robert Rich 2nd Earl of Warwick by whom they were alienated with the manor to the Cokes, the maternal ancestors of Viscount Melbourne. Bridges states that "the vicarage was ordained in the time of Hugh Wells. This endowment seems however to have been relinquished, and another ordained subsequently to the taxations of 1254 and 1291, as no vicarage is mentioned in either of those records. In the ecclesiastical survey or king's books, in 1535 it was valued at £6.11s10d per ann. deducting 3s for procurations". "A certificate from Northamptonshire", printed in 1641 describes "Duston, a poor Vicarage stipendiary neere Northampton. Master James the Vicar is well reputed but his living is very poore, only 20 pounds yearely some 5 pounds more was given lately by the Honourable Earle of Warwicke, but he having sold his estate there, "that Exhibition is discontinued". It is a discharged living, being certified under the act 5 Anne (1707) to be only of the clear value of £19.13.5d per ann. It has been twice augmented by Queen Anne's bounty in 1727 with £200 by lot, and in 1754 with another £200 to meet a donation of £200 from Lady Gower. In the return of lovings under £150 per ann in 1809, the Bishop of Peterborough certified it to be of the clear yearly value of £93.5s5d arising from glebe, augmentation, and surplice fees; and in 1814 it was exonerated from land tax by the commission appointed Geo 3 (1806) when it was entered of the clear yearly value of £133.17s. The vicarage now consists of 25 a 3r 32p allotted by the commissioners of inclosure in lieu of the glebe, and of all vicarial tithes and moduses or compositions 5 a.2r.3p in exchange with Lord Melbourne, under the inclosure act, for certain meadow land called Durham dyke, which had been purchased in 1724 with the first augmentation of £200: and 21a 1r 5p at Guredon, awarded under the act for inclosing that parish 20 Geo 3 (1780) for lands purchased in 1775 with the second augmentation and donation of £200 each.

Peveril's Way, near the junction of the Weedon and Duston Roads, as does Peveril Road in the village of Duston, derives its name from the above-mentioned William Peveril, a follower (some would have us believe, a son) of William the Conqueror to whom the manor of Duston was transferred from its former Saxon owner, in the years immediately following 1066. Bants Lane, contrary to popular opinion (on which the historian ever delights to trample!) is not named after the late Rev. Peake Banton, Vicar of Duston from 1863 to 1891. At the time of the Enclosure Award for Duston, in 1777, there was a Bantom's Lane, and this is no doubt the same. The only explanation of the name Bantom's Lane is that the Duston Lodge Farm, situated in that lane until it was partly demolished in 1937 and 1938, belonged for a considerable time to farmers named Bantom or Banton, for the 1847 Directory of Duston contains the name "G.F. Banton, farmer. (The Lodge". This Mr. G.F. Banton played an important part in Duston life during the last century and was for many years a Churchwarden of Duston. Strangely enough there seems to have been no relationship between him and the Rev. Peake Banton, although the name is an uncommon one.

Our historical wanderings next bring us to the Village War Memorial, which is on Weldon stone with steps in Derbyshire stone. At the first meeting called to consider the question of a memorial, held on September 4th 1919, it was suggested that it should take the form of a village hall or institute, with a Roll of Honour. E. Rogers, Bull, Esq, of Duston House, was appointed Chairman of the Committee, Mr. G.L. Faram, Hon Secretary, and Mr. W.P. Cross, of Oak Lodge, Hon Treasurer, The Hon Secretaryship rapidly passed to Mr. E.C. Trasler, and still later to Mr. A.R. Jones. At a meeting on February 5th, 1920, a memorial cross was decided upon instead of the Hall, owing to lack of support. Amongst the sites proposed was the piece of spare land at the junction of Melbourne Lane and Main Road, but on March 22nd, 1920, Mr. A.E. Smith, of Elms Farm, Millway, kindly promised to give a piece of his orchard, which was gratefully accepted. It is interesting to recall that in addition to the donations received, the balance on the Duston Peace Celebrations amounting to £18 14s 6d, was given to the fund. Other money was collected at a Concert given by the Northampton Volunteer Band on July 23rd, 1920, and the proceeds of another concert, and of a football match arranged by the Duston Football Club also swelled the fund. The total cost of the Memorial Scheme, including incidental expenses, was £248 8s. The Memorial, 11 feet high, designed and executed by Messrs. J.G. Pullen & Sons, was unveiled on Sunday, February 6th, 1921, at 3 p.m. by Lt. Col John Brown, D.S.O. Deputy Lieutenant of Northamptonshire, and was dedicated by the Rev. W.D. Pearson, M.A. (Vicar). The ceremony at the memorial was preceded by an impressive ceremony in the parish church, the chapel choir co-operating with the church choir in leading the singing. Mr C.H. Battle, as Superintendent of the Congregational Chapel, read the lesson, and the Vicar gave an address. In addition to officials already mentioned, the Committee included the Vicar, Messrs, G.H. Stevenson, A. Handscomb, F. Stow, A.E. Caborn, H. Mallard, O. Munday, D. Greenough, F. Adams, F. Harrison, A.B. Harrison, A.B. Jones and A. Adams. At a meeting on November 9th, 1921, the memorial was handed over as a public monument to the Parish, and vested in the custody of the Parish Council. In this connection it is interesting to note that on no less an authoritative production than the 1927 O.S. Map, this road was called Randolph Road, obviously after former 20th Century residents of Moray Lodge, but a name which never seems to have been used by parishioners. It is to be regretted that when other roads on the "Stevenson Estate" were constructed in the first decade of this century, they were not given more imaginative names than Ashwood, Beechwood and Sycamore Roads. Similarly the names Southfield Road, Westfield Road and Eldean Road, contain little or nothing of interest to the lover of local history. Very wisely, application was successfully made a few years ago for the name "Co-op Lane" to be changed once more to "Meeting Lane", thus recalling the fact that it was in this lane where those former parishioners who felt unable to "conform" to the services of the Parish Church, held their first religious meetings. Ryeland Road, constructed as recently as 1933 or 1934, was more happily named than some of the other modern roads in our parish, for the name "Ryeland" was applied many years ago to the greyish-brown stone found in the New Duston part of the parish. (The quarrymen, themselves, called it "The Roylands"). Although the origin of the name Port Road may be either from the Latin porto, I carry, or porta, a gate, Mr. B.S.J. O'Neill, of H.M. Office of Works, thought that the Port Roads to be found in various parts of the country are ancient pre-Roman trackways.

He also surmises that the road leading from Duston past Berrywood to Nobottle is a Roman Road, as there are distinct traces of Roman villas found on either side of this road in neighbouring parishes. In that case, the Berrywood – Nobottle Road and Port Road have existed side by side since Roman days.

Duston House is understood to be the Dower house for Upton Hall, and this supposition is almost certainly true, as the Colonel Samwell on whose instructions Duston House was build in 1820 – 1822, was no doubt a member of the Samwell family whose ancestor, Wn. Samwell purchased Upton in 1600 from Sir Richard Knightley, and members of which continued to reside at Upton, at least until 1841. It is also interesting here to record that about the year 1837, the Squirrels Inn was owned by Frances Samwell (a connection of Lord Nelson) of Duston House, and that this Inn was, without doubt, so named because the arms of the Samwell Family.

The Old Village

The cottages looking out on to what remains of the village green were originally the parish workhouses, as shown by the name, "Workhouse Yard" still given them. This mention of the village workhouse reminds us that before the Poor Law System was inaugurated, the preaching of charity sermons was a great feature in the churches of our land. In this connection the shortest sermon on record is said to have been preached by the famous Dean Swift. His text was "He that hath pity upon the poor lendeth unto the Lord, and that which he hath given will be repaid to him again." The sermon on that text ran as follows, "Now my friends, you hear the terms of the loan. If you like the security, down with the cash!" It is not known when the Duston workhouse was built, but we do know that an Act of Parliament of 1723 authorised vestries (the forerunners of Parish Councils), to build workhouses. Before this date, the erection of each new one required special legislation.

Some vestries still granted outdoor relief, but others forced the poor into "The House". The parish overseer's duty of looking after those in "The House" or in receipt of outdoor relief was not an easy one. There is a true story of an overseer who was appointed to the office all unbeknown to him. However he accepted the office like a lamb, but the vestry was amazed and indignant to find that he gave orders for relief to everyone who called at his door and asked for it. He did not mean to get his head broken by refusing! "If anybody comes to me for an order I shall give him one". Needless to say the vestry soon relieved him of the troublesome office.

An interesting document which reads as follows:

"To Robert Newton a Constable in the City of London, and also to all Constables and other officers of the peace whom is may concern, and to the Churchwardens and Overseers of the Poor of the Parish of Dosham (Duston), near Northampton in the County of Northampton or either of them to receive and obey.

Whereas Mary Ann Storey was on the 20th day of January inst. apprehended in the Parish of St. Lawrence Jewry in the City of London, and whereas the said Mary Ann Storey hath been by John Boydell Esq. one of the Aldermen of the City of London and one of his Majesty's Justices of the Peace in and for the said City, examined and adjudged and convicted to be a Rogue and Vagabond, and hath in consequence of such conviction, been committed to and confined in Bridewell Hospital, for the space of seven days pursuant to the Statures in that made and provided. And whereas upon examination of the said Mary Ann taken before me this day upon Oath (which examination is hereunto annexed) it doth appear that the last legal settlement of the said Mary Ann is in the said Parish of Dosham. These are therefore to require you the said Robert to convey the same Mary Ann to the Parish of St. Botolph with Aldersgate in the Co. of Middlesex that being the first Parish in the next Precinct through which she ought to pass in the direct road to the said parish, to which she is to be sent, and to deliver her to the constable or other officer of such first Parish in such next Precinct, together with this Pass and Examination of the said Mary Ann take his Receipt for the same. And the said Parish of Dosham there to be delivered to some Churchwarden, Chapel-warden, or Overseer of the Poor to be provided for according to law, and you said Churchwardens. Chapel-wardens and Overseers of the Poor are hereby required to receive the said Mary Ann and provide for her according to Law. Given under my hand and seal, the 27th Day of January in the year of our Lord 1798.

A separate sheet among our parish "papers" reads "The Examination of Mary Ann Storey a Rogue and Vagabond apprehended in the City of London before the one of His Majesty's Justices of the Peace for the said City, this 27th Day of January, 1798.

Who on her Oath saith, that her parents have informed her which information she believes to be true that she was born in the Parish of Dosham near Northampton in the County of Northampton. And hath not obtained a subsequent settlement to this examiner's knowledge or belief.

Taken and sworn the Day and Year first above written before me.

MARY ANNE (her X mark)
JOHN BRYDELL
(N.B. one who was unable to sign her own name could hardly be expected to spell the name of our village correctly).

Also among our Parish "Papers" are (1) An account served on the Parish Officers of Duston in 1816 by Robt. Abbey & Son, touching the settlement of G.T. and his family, amounting to £17 0s 3d. Obviously they had been living in another parish (it was Dallington) which objected when they became chargeable on the Poor Rate there, and so the Duston Officers had after due scrutiny, had them back in Duston, to which parish they belonged. (2) An account to the Overseers of the Parish of Duston. 1832 rendered by Robt. Hewitt "In Jolley's Settlement". It starts off "March 14th, Jolley and his wife and family having been removed from your Parish to Ecton by orders. Attending you when you informed me you thought the orders would be appealed against etc etc… 6s 8d. Later it goes on "Understanding that the late Col. Samwell, the pauper's master always entered the particulars of his hirings in a book and considering such entries might be of service to our case, journey to Duston to Mrs. Samwell, the widow of the late Colonel to examine such book and taking long extract therefrom and collecting other evidence…£1 1s 0d. Their total account came to £42.10s 8d for eventually the case was tried at the Court of Quarter Sessions. Still another "Paper" is an order dated 1800, for Thomas Thompson and Ann his wife and Elizabeth their daughter and Clement their son. Clement their son to be moved back to Brixworth from Duston because they had become chargeable to Duston Parish.

There are also indentures of Apprenticeship of Poor Children of various dated between 1802 and 1830. One dated May 22nd, 1802, tells how Thomas Botterill aged 13 years was apprenticed to W.N. Dawkins of the Parish of St. Peters, Northampton. Cordmaker, "until he shall accomplish his full age of 21 years". He was placed in this apprenticeship by John Hilliard the eldest, and Robert Blewitt as Churchwardens of Duston and John Hilliard, the elder and John Facer as Overseers of the Poor of Duston. From the Indenture we also learn that Dawkins "shall and will during all the Term aforesaid find, provide and allow for the apprentice, competent and sufficient meat, drink, apparel, lodging, washing and other things necessary and fit for an Apprentice. (Provided that the said Convenant shall continue in force for no longer than 3 calendar months).

In 1800 approximately 68½% of the rates were used for the relief of the poor. Later payments include J.A., a sheet, 5s 8d; Jos Smith for tracking, £3 4s; Pd the parish of Houghton for T.G.'s wife and family, £4; For J.A.'s funeral, 4s; A pair of stockens for M.B., 1s 10d; Aug 3 1805, Paid the sub, to the Hospital (earliest mention), £3 3s pd Richardson for bringing S.B. from Brackley, 8s; July 19, 1806; paid for a letter from London, 7d; Paid John Green for burying N's child, 1s; To bedtick for Sarah Forstes; 8s 6d; Pd towards repairing J.D.'s house, £12; Dec 4 1807, lace Pillar and bobings for S.B. 3s; Paid Samual Law, Premium for M.B. (she was appointed to him) £5; Jan 29 1808 Paid Mrs. Hollowell for Beer for the Masons, 3s 7d; April 1st 1808, paid John Sail in the Infirmary 7s; May 28 1808, pd Dr. Clark for attending "x" 10s 6d (first observed case where doctor actually so called); Feb 17, 1810, Paid Martha Harris fore curing S.E.'s leg, 5s; June 2nd, 1810, Wm. Jonson for 700 of bricks. £1 8s; to J.S. for his wife and children, he being in the local (prison?) 15s to W.N. for medson for his wife when ill, 5s; May 20th 1811, Paid T.L. Lock (local) militia, 10s; Paid the expense without moving S.E. to Kislingbury (evidently he was a burden on the Duston rates, and so was moved to his own parish); Paid the expense with T.C. who was found drowned, £21; May 15 1813, paid for fetching lime and sand for poor houses; 4s; May 28th 1813, Pd Saml. Mellows for Painting the Poor Houses. £5 0s 5d; June 19. Saml. Mellows for Whitewashing, 4s; July 23, 1813, paid Mary Nobles for cleaning the workhouse;

An old Overseer's Book, 1803 to 1819, gives much interesting information about Duston during the last twelve years of the time England was fighting Napolean, and for four years after the end of the war, when England was in a very bad way owing to unemployment. Among the many payments made by the Overseer, and mentioned in this book, are the following; To Thorns for the Workhouse garden hedge, 2s 6d Paid for the Easter dinner (no doubt, of those in the workhouse) £3 14s; Register Book for Apprentices, 5s; For pot links for the workhouse, 1s 6d; to tea-kettle for ditto, 4s; Paid for a grate for the workhouse, 4s 9d Saml. Mellowe's Mason Bill (probably for work at the workhouse, £1 8s 8d; to a bottle of straw (perhaps for a bed), 6d; To a coat, waistcoat and breeches and hat and smock frock for T.C. £1 15s; To 5 ells of cloth at 1s 5d per ell, for T.C., 7s 1d; Paid D.T. 3s., James Jones' bill for shoes, £1 3s 8d; To a pair of shoes for G.M., 8s Paid a woman for nusinge, 4s; Total expenses for the year, April 1803, to April, 1804 are entered as; Overseer £274 9s 7d; Constable's bill (93 3s 1½d; Churchwarden's bill £12 16s 10d; Overseers of the Highway £20 19s 10d.

One of the Duston Parish Charities is called "Facer's Dole". The following is an extract from the donor's will; "last will and testament of John Facer late of Duston in the County of Northampton yeoman, deceased, duly executed in the presence of and attested by five witnesses bearing date the third day of July, one Thousand six hundred and forty four… I give and bequeath to the Poore of Duston, tenne shillings of good and lawful money of England yearly and every yeare to be paid out my said lande and tenement in Kislingbury aforesaid for ever upon the said seven the twentieth day of December".

A communication from the Charity Commission tells us that in 1825 the land at Kislingbury was in the occupation of a Mr. Thomas Linnell. In 1852 "Facer's Dole" Land was sold by Richard Linnell to H. Howes, Solicitor of Northampton who in turn sold it to Mr. R.C. Westley of Milton. A communication from the Charity Commissioners dated 22nd February 1881 authorised legal proceedings against "Mr. R.C. Westley or owner" of Facer's Charity Land in Kislingbury to enforce payment of the annual sum of ten shillings due. The writer was informed in the late 1930's that although the 10s per year was still forthcoming no one could identify the land. In 1837 out of the proceeds of Reynold's Charity (described in pebble 12) and Facer's Dole, 23 widows and widowers received 1s 6d each. In 1838, 1839 and 1840 the sum of £2 2s 0d was paid out in money to 20 widows and widowers at 1s 6d each. This sum was made up of £1 6s 8d from J. Barker, Earls Barton (Reynold's Charity). 10s from Thomas Linnell (Facer's Dole) and 5/4 paid out of the Church Sacrament Offerings. On or near St. Thomas's Day, December 21st, 1943 the Poor's Close, Charity Money was distributed to deserving parishioners in Duston and Duston – St. James. It is reasonable to suppose that this distribution in former days in coal or other kind, has been made annually at that same season, ever since the parish of Duston was "enclosed" by the Act of Parliament on February 20th, 1777. Until that year the land of the parish of Duston, like that of almost every parish in England, had been divided into three large fields together with a piece of common land on which latter every parishioner had the right to cut turf, furze, gorse, etc. The three fields in Duston were Arbour Field (lying towards Dallington and St. James) Langdold Field and Middle Field. When Duston was "enclosed" (ie. the tree fields were divided into smaller ones of the size owe now know) the Enclosure Commissioners (Thomas and John Oldknow of Nottingham, James King of Daventry and Tresham Chapman, of Old) made this interesting award; "To the Vicar, Churchwardens and Overseers of Duston – that part of the land lying on the Heath called Strawberry Leys containing 12 acres, 1 rood, 33 perches, including 2 acres, 1 rood 33 perches allowed for roads and ways in, though and over the same – for the industrious poor of Duston in lieu (place) of the right of the poor to cut, turf, furze and gorse bushes for fuel, on or upon the Heath and Waste Grounds". Strawberry Leys, now called Poor's Close (field) is a three-cornered field lying to the right of Sandy Lane, New Duston, as one proceeds from Port Road towards the Nobottle Road, and it is the rent derived from the letting of this field which is still distributed. Baker's copy of the Abstract of Returns of Charitable Donations reveals that in 1787 the income derived from Poor's Close was £10 a year, but "at a vestry held this 15 day of April, 1811" the field was let to Mr. Charles Whiting for a lease of seven years at £20 a year. By 1837 "Thos Tressler and Jo Seal" were paying £30 a year rent for it, and it is interesting to learn that on January 17th 1838, Mr. T. Daniel, Bugbrooke Wharf, was paid £23 13s 5d for 437 cwt. of coal purchased from the Poor's Close money and which was distributed to various people.

The other part of "Ferndale" was formerly the "Old Wooden Spout Inn". What a glorious name for a village pub! In 1844 it was run by Robert Farmer, and in 1866, there was a Mrs. Farmer, beer retailer in Duston. No doubt this "Directory" entry refers to "old Bet Farmer", who is still remembered by old Dustonians as having kept this house. Among other things it is remembered by Old Dustonians as having kept this house. Among other things it is remembered that Bet bless her heart gave a free supper of mutton and turnips on the Friday of Feast Week each year. The last to keep "The Old Wooden Spout" was a Mr. Wooley probably the Mr. Joseph Woolley, who was also a carpenter. In this particular inn, the innkeeper had to descend a number of steps to draw of beer for his customers. Knowing this to be the case, the ironstone workers employed at that time in the Millway Fields, used to visit the "Spout" at intervals, one by one, sufficiently close to one another to cause the innkeeper to blow, and no doubt curse, as yet another half-pint was ordered! It must have been in 1874 that this house ceased to quench the thirst of the Duston yokels, for in that year we find that part of the house was converted for the use of the then village schoolmaster Mr. Greenwood, at a cost of £84 4s 9d. The other portion, nearer the vicarage, was occupied by the Vicarage gardener, who had no front entrance. The last schoolmaster to live in the divided house was Mr. A.T. Speight, and the last gardener, Mr Frank Faulkner. Eventually in the 1890s there was a fire, and thereafter until the Estate Sale on July 3rd 1919, the village schoolmaster continued to reside there in occupation of the whole house. Until 1896 the occupant was still Mr. Speight, and thereafter Mr. A.R. Jones.

Mr Perret of Duston in front of the old pond at Pond Farm, Old Duston.

1898

"Oak Lodge" Duston Main Rd, with huge oak tree in garden.

1885

Duston Main Road scene with children in their best Sunday clothes.

1960

Duston House Victorian Conservatory and glass domed billiard room.

1900

View from Church Way looking across Millway to Upton. Only one thatched cottage to be seen.

1920

Mr. G. Faulkner, Shepherd to Messrs. Radcliffe who farmed part of Holmleigh. After 1919 he lived in Melbourne Lane.

1930

Millway Cottages. These picturesque cottages in the 18th century were then Manor Cottages.

1935

Mr. Faulkner's bakers cart (under the tall elms) delivering in Millway.

1960

Bank Cottages East End with old monastic window which is believed to have come from the ruins of St James Abbey.

1948

Millway from School end.

1898

After Sunday morning service view of High St.

1888

Boys at play on the village green.

1926

Granny Hopewell's cottage, corner of Berrywood Road (demolished for road widening)

The old estate cottages in Melbourne Lane before Lord Cowper demolished them and rebuilt the present stone properties.

1908

View of Smiths Cottage from Millway.

1897

Chapel Lane looking on to Main Rd Chapel on right. Note pump on left.

1920

Harry Laws football team played in Mill Lane field. Photograph outside the old stone barn.

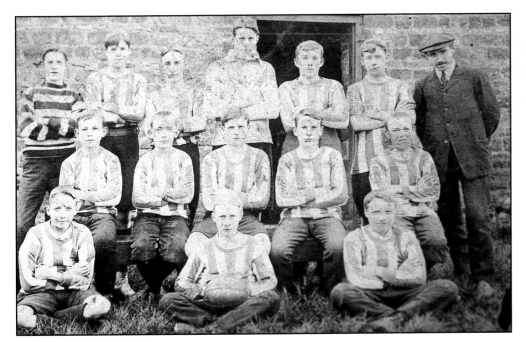

Part 2 – Village School

From an old Vestry Meeting book we learn that on September 1st, 1853, a meeting was called "for the purpose of considering the necessary steps to be taken in carrying on the works of the school already commenced". Those present included the Rev. R.H. Cox, in the chair, the Rev. F.S. Troman vicar of Dallington, to the school in whose parish Duston children were then going, and Mr. Law (architect). At this meeting it was proposed by Mr. J. Daniels and seconded by Mr. Hales (believed to be another farmer of the parish) that insomuch as education for the poor is a positive evil, we consider the proposed school at Duston wholly unnecessary". (The good old days!). An amendment was proposed and seconded "that in the opinion of this meeting a school for instructing the children of the poor at Duston is much needed". The Vicar, possibly anxious for the good men of Duston during the vicariate at the hands of some future local historian greedy for the information of a village squabble, here called on the proposer and seconder of the original motion to withdraw it, but delightful to record that they persisted in having it put from the chair! Needless to say they lost and the school was duly erected, the actual deed of conveyance of the site and premises of the Duston Church of England poor school, being sealed on December 7th, 1857.

The first teacher mentioned in the school accounts seems to be Mill Milon (or Mitson, the writing is not easily legible, who is entered as receiving £8.13s salary (for services rendered) from April to August 8th 1863. Miss Pierce who came from Northampton appears to have commenced duty on July 27th, 1863, at the princely salary of 9s per week and to have remained at the school until February 7th, 1873.

The first schoolmaster was Edward Wood, who, coming from a school in Oxford began work at Duston on July 7th, 1873. His wife came with him as his assistant but both were given three months notice on October 23rd, 1873. William Greenwood, the second headmaster came straight to Duston from his training at the National Society Training College at Battersesa, which he left in December 1873. He lived with his mother, first in the "1732 House" opposite the school, then later in the schoolmaster's cottage "Ferndale" no longer used as such but still has a name plaque on the porch entrance. After Mr. Greenwoods records in the minute book, continue entries of poor attendance of children. 1876 August 27th to 31st attendance 61 children gleaning in the fields, August 31st School closed for three weeks holiday, October 8th to 12th attendance picking potatoes, October 19th school closed as gas was being put in the school. February Mr. A. Speight was the next headmaster in 1877 attendance around 100 including 56 infants. I have the copy of an agreement of a teacher to a boy to the religious care of her pupils in accepting her responsibilities at the school in 1890 by Miss M. Gardam, daughter of the first farm manager of Berrywood Mental Hospital who married William Spokes of Upton Mill (Mr. John Spokes grandfather) there are some very interesting school lists of that time. Here is her letter to the Rev. Peak Banton accepting her responsibilities of Duston Church of England School in 1890.

"I hereby agree on condition of being paid thirty pounds a year in quarterly payment not in advance by the Vicar of Duston to undertake the office of Assistant Teacher at the Duston church school to assist in teaching the children of both sexes at such times and in such manner as the said Vicar shall direct. To attend and teach

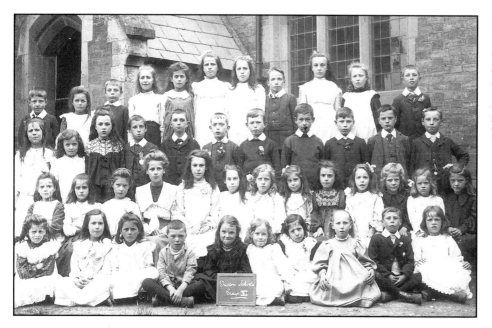

1906

Group 2 children from the age of 8 at Duston Village School with Mr. Jones, Headmaster. Another 50 in group 1 made up a total of some 80 children then being educated there.

in the Sunday School morning and afternoon, walk with the children to church, and sit with them during Divine Service. I also agree in case of illness not being able to attend to the duties of the school, to obtain and pay a substitute subject to the approval of the Vicar to whom the substitute shall first be referred, or else allow the Vicar to obtain to pay a substitute for me.

I also agree to give three months notice to the Vicar in writing if at any time I wish to end the agreement, three months notice in writing being also given to me by the Vicar if he at any time wishes to end this engagement."

Many of the Old Duston families are on the school list: Adams, Hopewells, Gardams, Dove, Mallards, Faulkner, Farmer, from the records of Mrs. Capell (nee Molly Spokes). A.R. Jones was like his predecessor deeply involved in affairs of the church, so many older people remember him with great affection. Some ten years ago I visited his two sisters in Northampton both in their eighties. He lived to be ninety three still residing in Duston. By 1900 the population of the village was rising, consequently more room was needed and Millway extension was built. The large window was removed on the south gable end of the old building and rebuilt on the new crucifer cross section, this was opened by Earl Cowper, Lord of the Manor, supported by the Bishop Sir Ronald and Lady Knightley and Mr. P. Phipps M.P., the Rev H.J. Wells composer of the hymn "At even ere the sun was set" preached at the thanksgiving service at St. Lukes in the afternoon. A.R. Jones continued through the great war doing great work in organising the village education through very difficult times, shortages of books etc, until a crises arose owing to the poor facilities at the school. Blacklisted by the board of Education, a meeting was held early in the year to see what the governors and clergy could do to end this uncertainty in the parish. Later in March the Archdeacon Oakham and Canon Williams were invited to address a meeting to really explain what could be done to avoid such a calamity. On October 17th a special meeting was held in the parish to raise the necessary money to recondition the school. A.R. Jones continued with his good work until 1932 and enjoyed his retirement in Duston where he died aged ninety three. A.E. Gawthorne was appointed as his successor when other additions were made to the school and new estates were being built, he and the Rev. Thompson the chairman of the school governors coped with the problem of evacuees coming and eventually the school having to cope with dividing the children up into half day classes. This ends Ray Lagden's most valuable contribution to this book.

Many innovations, visits to working sites, engineering etc. were all part of the schools curriculum in which my own children took part. Modernisation was to take place leaving the school very much as it is today. 1946 saw Mr. J.A. Monk taking over and conditions were that much better. Building of a new school in this area was about to commence and it would not be too many years before some eight more schools would take over the need of local expansion.

(F. Golby)

1890

Assistant teacher's letter to Duston vicar regarding to conditions of her employment.

1892 CHILDRENS ATTENDANCE SHEET AT DUSTON VILLAGE SCHOOL

Admission Number	Date of Admission. Mon. Yr.	Date of Birth. Mon. Yr.	At Last Inspect. Age last Birthd.	Stand. Present.	FIRST QUARTER NAME.	Half-Times	No. in Month	SCHOOL FEES. Jan M27	M3	M10	M17	M24	M31	Feb M7	M14	M21	M28	M7	M14	M21	School Times Carried forward	January M27 T	28 W	29 T	30 F	Attendances	M3	4 T	5 W	6 T	F	Attendances
					BROUGHT FORWARD.																										
2	246 77 5	42 1			Holton George	9		2	2	2	2	2	2	2	2	2	2			30											8
3	214 76 5	42 11			Smith Ernest	8		2	2	2	2	2	2	2	2	2	2			31											7
4	344 79 4	40 7			Walker Walter	10		2	2	2	2	2	2	2	2	2	2			24											10
5	250 77 6	43 6			Allen John	4		left																		left					
6	206 76 3	43 3			Dove Henry	7		x	4	2	2	2	2	2	2	2	2			38											10
7	235 76 5	43 5			Bishop George	7		3	3	3	3	3	3	3	3	3	3			39											7
8	244 77 4	44 3			Dove William	6		2	2	2	2	2	2	2	2	2	2			38											10
9	265 77 10	44 7			Billington Edward	6		2	2	2	2	2	2	2	2	2	2			30											10
10	257 77 6	43 6			Gary Samuel	7		3	3	3	3	3	3	3	3	3	3			28											8
11	122 78 10	43 10			Willet Joseph	7		2	2	2	2	2	2	2	2	2	2			34											10
12	285 78 5	44 1			Farmer George	7		2	2	2	2	2	2	2	2	2	2			36											10
13	234 76 12	43 12			Farmer Frederick	7		2	2	2	2	2	2	2	2	2	2			40											10
14	245 77 5	44 2			Harrison Charles	6		2	2	2	a	2	2	2	2	2	2			35											10
15	273 78 3	45 1			Alsop Henry	6		3	3	3	3	3	3	3	3	3	3			38											10
16	286 78 5	44 5			Hopewell Henry	6		3	3	3	3	3	3	3	3	3	3			39											10
17	359 80 3	46 1			Garratt Hector A	5		3	3	a	a	a	3	3	a	a	3	3	3	18											9
18	373 80 6	43 9			Darby Arthur	7		2	2	2	2	2	2	2	2	2	2			22											8
19	380 80 9	41 4			Liddington William	9		2	2	a	2	2	2	a	2	2	a			22											6
20	287 78 5	44 5			Bishop Wm Warren	6		2	2	2	2	a	2	2	2	2	2			31											9
21	304 78 4	45 4			Purnell Albert	5		2	2	2	a	2	2	2	2	2	2			25											8
22	337 79 6	44 4			Poole William	6		2	2	a	a	2	2	2	2	2	2			13											7
23	389 81 1	43 3			Stokes Samuel	7					4	4	4	4	left					2											
24					Booth Charles												x	8												
25																				1569											

1892 Childrens' attendance sheet at Duston Village School

Duston People

1919

Robert Errington outside his Millway garden shed, he bought land at New Duston in the 1919 Estate Sale and gave part of it for Errington Park.

1907

Mr. William Bailey (whose son William emigrated to Canada 1907) with his beehives at Pump Cottage, Millway.

1910

Duston roadmen Mr. Lawrence and Mr. Adams outside Smiths cottage off Millway.

1939

Blind Billy Jeyes outside the barn doors at the Wilcox Farm (wartime notices on display).

1936

Duston Darby and Joan outing included Mrs. Bennett, Mrs. Faulkner, Mrs. Black, Mrs. Wright, Mrs. Bonner, Mr. Paul, Mr. Laughton, Mrs Green, Mr. Rice.

1942

Duston Home Guard after Church Parade.

Duston Village Institute

It was a great occasion for Duston when on December 21st 1923 the village institute was opened in memory of Duston men who lost their lives in World War I. A distinguished committee led by W.P. Cross (chairman) a leather manufacturer who lived at Dallington who took great interest in Duston affairs. Although only a first war surplus wooden building said to have come from a prisoner of war camp at Eastcote it has been indispensible to village life here for so many years continually cared for by a local committee. First a mens club was started. Two billiard tables were installed, then Duston womens institute was formed, various evening classes were held and regular dances on a Saturday night became a popular venue for young people. For some 50 years this was used as a church hall for all their indoor functions, harvest festival suppers for concerts, plays etc. It was the local point of village activities.

1923

The opening of the village institute (hall) December 21st, 1923, *Seated left to right:* Percy Major (Hon. Treas.), W.P. Cross (President), Lyrdd Wilson Stevenson, *Standing:* Mr. A. Smith, Mr. E.A. Trasler, J.W. Fisher, J.P. Harrison (JP), Horace Faulkner, F. Spencer, E. Malure, E. Cowley, G. Gordon, Mr. O. Mundy, Mr. F. Billing, Mr. F. Billingham, Mr. C.B. Jolley, Mr. E.R. Jones, Mr. J.F. Stopps, Mr. G.H. Law.

1956

Children's party at the village institute included Les Worral, Paul Hopewell, Philip Odell, Peter Smith, Ian Flinders, David Chadrach, John Reynolds, Nick Short, David Masters, Sandra Swain, Rita Bardons, Richard Mallard, Roger Mallard, Wanda Sawford.

1945

Hodgson's Stores next to the village institute.

1947

Snow bound main road near bottom shop Duston.

1960

Mr. Skinner's wireless and television premises, Melbourne Lane.

1960

Harvest Festival Supper in village institute.

Front Table left to right: D. Allaway, A. Allaway, A. Dransfield,
D. Whitlock, Nicholas Whitlock, Michael Reynolds, Paul Ager, Paul Beesley, Phil Kidsley.

The second table: Hazel Bandy, Mr. and Mrs. Bandy, Mrs. Reynolds, Chris Sergeant, Mr. Sergeant, Mrs. Mundy, Jill Dorricot, Roger Dove, Mrs. Dove, Mrs. Watts, John Favell.

1923

Village institute when erected.

Village Shops

1913

Village stores showing Old Baptist Chapel.

1947

Mr. and Mrs. Adams outside the wine shop in Old Duston.

1940

Mr. Percy Faulkner on his delivery round in the village.

1930

Harpole Co-Op Society Stores corner of Meeting Lane, Mr. Rogers and Mr. Wright.

1898

Cobblers shop. Main Rd, Duston.

3 Duston Estate Village Farms. Sold 1919

Holmleigh Farm

Coloured Red on Plan No. 1.

A VERY ATTRACTIVE FARM

known as

HOMELEIGH FARM

Situate in the Parish of Duston and fronting the Main Street, with an Area of about

298 acres

Including Excellent Arable and Pasture Land stretching down to the **Nene** and with a very well situated

GOOD FARM HOUSE

Containing:—On the Ground Floor—Porch into Entrance Hall, opening **on** to Lawn, Drawing Room, Dining Room, Office, Dairy, Pantry with boarded floor, Kitchen with Cupboards, Back Kitchen, Sink with hot and cold water. Back and Side Entrances.

On the First Floor—5 Bedrooms, and a Dressing Room, good cupboards; Bath Room with Basin and Hot and Cold Water laid on. W.C.

Outside :—Yard with Large Underground Soft Water Tank and Pump. Coal house and W.C. Pump. Good Kitchen Garden, Orchard and Lawn.

THE FARM BUILDINGS

Which are substantial and well built,

Consist of:—Wash House near back door with Sink, Turnip House, Mixing Shed and Cooling House with brick floor, Cow House for 12, Cow House for 4, 5-Bay open Shed for about 12 Bullocks with Yard, Chaff House, Cart Horse Stable for 7, Nag Stable with 2 loose boxes and Loft over with Outside Stairs, Pump and Drinking Trough in Yard.

Opposite—Harness Room and Coach House or Motor House with Loft over, 2 Pigsties, 6-Bay open Shed with Yard and Drinking Trough, Fowl House at back. 4-Bay open Shed adjoining for about 8 with Yard and Drinking Trough, Loose Box with tying for 5, and Barn with Stone Floor. Adjoining, 5-Bay open Cart Shed with 5th Bay boarded in for Trap House. Large Rickyard with 5-Bay Dutch Barn and small Garden with close railed fence.

Another range of Farm Buildings adjacent, originally belonging to another Farm, consists of :—Large Rickyard with Pump and Drinking Trough supplying other troughs from overflow ; 6-Bay Cart Shed, Stone and Thatched; Brick and Slate Barn with good Stone Floor, Loose Box with tying for 5, 9-Bay open Shed with Yard, divided into 3 Sheds of 3 Bays each with Yard and Drinking Trough for each, Loose Box with

Rose Cottage

Coloured Pink on Plan No. 1.

THE VALUABLE ACCOMMODATION HOLDING

known as

ROSE COTTAGE

Situate in the Village of Duston at the entrance from Northampton, and containing an Area of about

79 acres

Of Accommodation Arable and Pasture Land, with Valuable Frontages.

THE FARM HOUSE

Of Stone and Tile, is on the Main Street, and contains:—On the Ground Floor—Drawing Room and Dining Room, Lobby, Kitchen with Hot and Cold Water laid on to sink, Larder, Cellar.

On the First Floor—2 Large Bedrooms and 1 smaller, Bathroom.

On the Second Floor—2 Bedrooms and Box Room.

Outside Verandah, with Kitchen and Side Doors opening into it, and communicating with Washhouse.

THE FARM BUILDINGS

Consist of—Coach House, Harness Room, Loose Box, 3-stall Stable, Loose Box, Mixing House, 3-bay open Shed with tying for 7, and Yard. 3-bay Dutch Barn. Stone and Slate Threshing Barn with brick and boarded floor. Wood and Iron 3-bay Cart Shed, 2 bays open, 1 closed. Loose Box and Pigsties with Iron Roof. Stone and Thatch Loose Box, Fowl House, Meal House. Rain-water trough.

Estate Yard Buildings including :—Brick and Tile Workshop with small Yard, 3-bay open Shed for Storing Material, and Yard.

Enclosure No. 77—Excellent Stone and Tiled Buildings with Walled-in Yard, consisting of Barn with brick and concrete floor, 2-bay open Shed into Yard with tying for 5, 2-bay open Shed into Field. Cow House with tying for 4.

THE LAND

Consists of about 51 acres of Arable Land and about 27 acres of Pasture Land, close to the Village and with good Frontages.

Ord. No.	Description.	Area.
73	Arable	10.404
77	Pasture and Buildings	10.263
Pt. 80	Arable	8.001
Pt. 81	Pasture	10.481
Pt. 148	House, Buildings, &c.	.020
Pt. 151	Roadway	.200
152	Pasture	4.787
153	Do.	1.091
183	Arable	9.163
185	Do.	2.289
Pt. 190	Do.	9.000
	In the occupation of Mr. W. Wilcox.	66.599
76	Arable	10.109
80	Do.	2.00
	In the occupation of Mr. W. Hillson.	12.159
Pt. 148	Pt. in hand pt. let to the Northampton Electric Light Co. (Power House).	120

Elms Farm

known as

THE ELMS FARM

In the Parish of Duston, with the Farm House and part of the Buildings in Duston Village, 2 miles from Northampton, and including some Excellent Meadow Land running down to the River Nene, having an area of about

83 Acres

THE FARMHOUSE

Which is built of Stone and Slate, contains:—On the Ground Floor—Dining Room, Drawing Room, Hall, Kitchen, Scullery, Pantry, Dairy and Pump House.

On the First Floor, approached by 2 staircases from Hall and Kitchen—4 Bedrooms, Bathroom with cupboards, Cold Water laid on, and W.C.

On the Second Floor—2 Large Attics with Fireplaces, and 1 without.

Water from Force Pump in Pump House. Soft Water to sink in Scullery.

Outside E.C. and Coal House. Garden Shed with open front.

Good Garden and Orchard.

THE FARM BUILDINGS

Near the House are chiefly of Stone and Slate, and include Mixing House with Loft over, Cowhouse with tying for 5 cows and Cowhouse for 6. Loose Box, 5-bay open Cart Shed, 2-bay open Shed with tying for 5 cattle. Double Pigsty. Large Carthorse Stable for 4 with space for fodder and Loft over, Loose Box, Fowl-house, Nag Stable for 2 and Coachhouse.

In Enclosure No. 207, Brick and Tile 3-bay open Shed, with Loose Box at end for about 10 Cattle.

In Enclosure No. 208. Brick and Slate Cowhouse with tying for 29 cows, and in Enclosure No. 209 Brick and Slate Cowhouse or Stable for about 7 cows or 5 horses, with shut-off Stall at end.

Pond and 2 Drinking Places supplied from Spring.

Also

LARGE COTTAGE AND GARDEN

Of Brick and Slate, and with the following accommodation—Front Room, Living Room, Office, Kitchen and Pantry, 3 Bedrooms, Outside E.C. Good Garden.

Enclosure No. 208 is part of the old Ironstone Quarry, and the present Cowhouse was originally the Iron Ore Co.'s Tram Shed, and the Cottage the Foreman's house.

Adjoining the Farm Buildings, and opening into the Duston Main Street,

TWO COTTAGES AND GARDENS

Built of Stone, with thatched roofs, and containing in No. 1, originally 2 cottages, Living Room, Kitchen and Scullery, Living Room, Pantry, with 2 Bedrooms over. Outside Coal House and Shed with Loft over. E.C.

No. 2, Kitchen and 2 Bedrooms, Outside Lean-to Shed with Sink. Washhouse. E.C. Water laid on.

6

Law's Newsagents

I am very privileged to include this collection of family photos of the village newsagents who for 3 generations delivered papers etc. and operated the Post Office in Old Duston.

1914

Harry Law outside his fathers paper shop in Sycamore Road, Duston.

1920

Mr. George Law's mother photographed in front of the institute.

1920

Harry Law's father's paper shop in Sycamore Road, Duston.

1916

Scout group: Bert Farmer, Cyril Smith, Ron Cowley, photographed at Tiffield.

1906

Harry Law's sisters Gladys and Ann.

Fred Law aged 4 outside his family home in Sycamore road.

1916

Village football, boys playing in field, the back of Ashwood Road (now Timken) with Ted Amos, Harold York, Aubrey Clark.

1920

Outside Holmleigh Farm, Gladys Law, Winnie Smith, Bertrum Smith.

1920

Duston young people enjoying an outing on the Nene in Northampton.

1926

Old Duston United football team playing on their pitch opposite the Vicarage now houses.

Aircraft that crash landed at Berrywood during 1914-1918 War.

1916

3 Duston boys photographed at Tiffield, Northants. Bert Farmer, Cyril Smith and Ron Cowley.

1920

In their Sunday best, Alice Smith, Bertrum and Winnie.

1918

Duston young men.

Standing- G. Harrison, Arthur Walton, Fred Adams, George Mallard, Percy Adams.
Seated- Freddie Smith, Albert Smith, Bernie Smith.

1918

Sergeant Brown.

1920

Duston paper boy outside
Harlestone House Stables.

Farms and Cottages

HOLMLEIGH FARM

Anyone with gardens in the Eastfield area will know how useless it is to dig or fork this clay soil in the winter months. Millway and Mill Lane was easy, light, sandy ironstone land, and it could be worked all winter. Here was another large part of the Holmleigh Farm, ideal for sowing winter corn. A strong shire horse could plough one acre a day. At the 1919 sale most of this great farm was sold up. In the 1930's the farm and buildings were in a very poor condition, the land and especially the buildings. Many of the stone barns etc. are now converted to pleasant residential properties now called Holmleigh Close. A lot of Mill Lane was bought in 1919 by the government to make available by the local authority for ex-servicemen, small holdings together with a sum of £100 each for one acre. When my father was invalided out of the army in 1919 all these small holding schemes had ended and he began his nursery on one acre, writing at this time, we are awaiting notice to quite the old nursery site in Mill Lane to begin the expansion of Northampton West to Upton.

Holmleigh Farm opposite the village school now the only converted stone property to remain, was a huge farm complex, farming for 300 acres. Cottages were all around the east side of the village for its 30 or more workers right round Meeting Lane. The lane around Pond Farm a hundred years ago, also part of the area in the estate sale of 1919, shows a total of four acres of farm cottages and buildings. The late Vince Smith who worked on the farm before 1914 for Mr. Jones, talked to me many years ago about his working life with the horses there. Then some 300 acres were under the plough, then so much of the land was in the now Eastfield area as far at Harlestone Road. Very heavy clay land (3 horse land) 3 horses were chained one behind the other, walking in the open furrows so not to tread the surface land hard, led by a boy to help turn the team at the end of a 15 foot headland, a lot of field beans were grown for all the horses as a winter crop, another 3 horse team would follow the first team with a bean sowing box fixed on to the plough, giving a spring cultivating row of some 26" to two furrows. It was good wheat land but after the ploughing the land had to be kept until after the winter frosts, and the heavy land had dried out, then he said wheat was sown by hand and it was possible for one horse to pull a light set of harrows over it.

WEGGS FARM

An isolated farm on the extreme and north west boundary of the parish off Sandy Lane, and now the large housing area off New Duston. In the 1919 estate sale described in the catalogue as follows:-

"New Duston building land 83 acres (then extending on to Duston Road fields opposite the then chapel) only 13 acres of arable land, 10 acres of pasture owing to the very heavy clay soil." Although the farm house is rather small, living room, kitchen, two bedrooms, outside water plumbing. The farm buildings were extensive, large barns etc. including a substantial granary which should have been left standing for conversion to be used by the new estate. In 1919 the farm was bought by Linnel Bros. It was known as Sandy Lane Farm. In 1948 Mr. Wegg purchased it and by 1956 Mr. Kimbell, the son in law, took it over and from then until its closure Mr. Coleman lived there as tenant and worked the farm. The isolation of the area is recalled by Mr. Burt who was there as a boy on the farm in 1947. In the winter of 1947 he had to walk across the fields to the shops and to attend worship Sunday by Sunday in the small Anglican church. A way of life for the small New Duston community.

ELMS FARM

Elms Farm is remembered for the huge elms that stood along that part of Millway, 79 acres. I remember the farm taking and bringing milking cows one mile each day to and from the meadow fields along the river. The row of farm-workers cottages on the corner of Millway were pulled down in the 1950's for the widening of the road.

Mr. Smith who farmed and purchased Elms Farm at the 1919 sale continued to farm until 1956 when it was sold to British Timken as was Holmleigh and Rose Cottage. Mr. Smith moved to Harlestone where his son Barry Smith still carries on farming. Goughs Cottages were built by a former tenant of Elms Farm around 1880.

DUSTON LODGE FARM

Duston Lodge Farm of 157 acres stood at the lower part of Bants Lane, a fine farmhouse and range of farm buildings being the nearest site to the expanding St. James area. It was advertised as all land buildings suitable for building sites between the wars, it was soon developed down to the Red House, but north of Bants Lane not until after 1945. These buildings and land were purchased by King & Co. of Blisworth, Ratcliffe and Jeffery the Northampton Brewery Co. of Bridge Street were tenants of this farm, also nearly 100 acres of other grazing land on the estate prior to the sale. Most of Lodge Farm was built on by 1939.

BANK COTTAGE

Originally built of plain uncut Duston stone removed it is said from the remains of the St. James Abbey, which was a Duston stone yard for a century or more. Bank cottage is indeed 16th century. When the present owner completely refurbished the interior from four separate cottages, the inner walls showed access from one room to the other, so originally the whole was one farm dwelling. In the the centre of it a huge chimney. At its base some eight feet square rising to a narrow chimney at the top. A fireplace and ingle nook was exposed after removing a plaster screen, on either side were found two cupboards some 2 and a half feet square, these I found out after some researching, were dry salt cupboards, the leather hinges still intact. On the east end of the house an upstairs medieval stone framed window, said to have come from the Abbey was removed for renovation but was in too poor a condition to be returned to its place. In the catalogue of each of the original cottages they had one room downstairs, two bedrooms, outside w.c. and a wash house at the rent of £5.00 each per annum.

BROOK COTTAGE

In New Duston so many stone properties have regrettably been pulled down, here is the story of one of them.

For many years I used to visit Mrs. Heywood in the picturesque cottage "Brook Cottage". The Harpole brook forming the boundary of the Duston parish, went on to the lake in Harlestone Park, to Dallington lakes and piped most of the way into the branches of the Nene, via Victoria Park. Brook Cottage had its origins in being built of the very hard stone from slate quarry. This stone was split by hand after being exposed to the winter, and used like the Collyweston stone of this county. Little remains to be seen in this area. I photographed an interesting garden edging of this material before it was redeveloped. Also in the garden, a "Milestone" with a cast iron plate featuring a cast iron shield marking the parish council boundary of Brixworth and Hardingstone, made at the Eagle Foundary, Northampton. The old stone part of the building was originally for the slate workers and stables. Then in early Victorian time, as this type of roofing was no longer required for local needs, the brick additions were added to the property and so made habitable. Alas this property has now been pulled down to make way for a housing estate.

1900

Bank Cottage
(on left of picture).

Main St, Duston.

62

Old Duston Houses

DUSTON HOUSE

Duston House was built in 1822 as a Dower House for the Samwell family who lived in Upton Hall for 250 years. This Dower House estate of some 30 acres, although in Duston Parish, was at some time added on to the Samwell land part of Upton which was over 2,000 acres in extent. Berrywood was originally sold away in 1876 for a lunatic asylum owing to the estate's insolvency after some 30 years of court proceedings concerning claimants to the estate as their was no direct heir. A private carriageway ran parallel to the old Weedon Road from Upton, then crossed over to Berrywood Lodge cottages direct to the Dower House. The house on Duston Road has a sombre classical appearance but on the West side is a delightful, elegant Georgian frontage inside adorned with Samwell coats of arms a complete replica of the improvements taking place on the West front of Upton House, at that time both properties bearing the dates and initials T.S.W.S. on the down pipes. Thomas Samwell Watson Samwell who assumed the title in 1790.

The Squirrels Public house is said to have derived its name from Samwell coat of arms which shows two squirrels Sejant-Addosed-Gules (sitting-back to back-Red) the house being next door to the old estate. The first publican is shown as Jonathan Harrison, 1845. It is thought that a claimant to Upton Estate, Mrs. L. Smith, lived at Duston House until the whole 2,000 acres and all the property was sold in 1864, William Butlin then acquired the Duston estate and lived there from 1861–1879 (the full story of him is recorded). Benjamin West then lived there till Mr. Muscott bought it in 1906 (Muscott Lane is named after him) he built two fine brick houses with local bricks in what was then the park (they are now part of Saxon Rise).

In 1907 Mr. and Mrs. Bull newly married (Mrs. Bull was the daughter of Sir Henry Randall) came to Duston and made their home at the Dower House for twenty years as tenants to Mr. Muscott who then moved to one of his newly built brick houses. In 1927 Mr. Major of Smith, Major & Stevens and T.E. Manning (Brewer) formed a syndicate and purchased the whole Duston Park Estate. Mr. Major retained the park and built himself "Ashtrees" in 1930, the large stone house is still there. He also later built a sizable mushroom farm in a corner of the park which was successfully managed by Mr. Faulkner who was a keen gardener. Mr. Major persuaded him to leave his works at St. James, this enterprise ended when Mr. Major died. His widow continued to reside in one of the Muscott houses by then known as the Highfield Houses. Redevelopment came to most of this area from Millway to Berrywood Road, including all his land. Mr. and Mrs. Bull decided to release much of their very large grounds adjoining, still maintaining and cultivating their flower gardens. Elizabeth their daughter still lives in part of the house, and, having known her for a long time I am very indebted to her for all her help in tracing the history and dates of Duston Dower House.

WILLIAM BUTLIN – IRONMASTER

The great ironmaster William Butlin lived in Duston House from 1861–1879. Duston House was built as a Dower House for the Samwell family who lived at Upton House from 1600–1845. The estate was eventually sold including Berrywood Farm for a mental hospital so William Butlin acquired this splendid Georgian property, he was indeed a wealthy man with his large works at Wellingborough and later owning the Hunsbury Hill Furnaces in 1876. The people, years ago, remembered Mr. Butlin's groom having to get his horse and carriage outside the drive each morning to convey him to the Bridge Street station by 8.00 a.m., then meet him at 4.30 p.m. from the Wellingborough train. He died in 1897 and is laid to rest in a huge white tiled vault over which is a huge metal anchor embedded in granite, made at his works. I was fortunate enough some 15 years ago to meet William's great grandson who kindly sent me his following written history of the family:-

The Butlin family is said to have descended from William de Boutevylein who in 1143 founded Pipewell Abbey at Pipewell, Northamptonshire, six miles from Kettering, for Cistercian monks.

The connecting link between Boutevylein and Butlin used to be found in the south aisle of Guilsborough Church in 1791, according to John Bridge, bore the following inscription:

"Here lyeth the body of Francis Butvelin, alias Butlin, of Hollowell, Kent, who departed this life September 14th, 1680" and *"Here lyeth the body of John Butlin, of Hollowell, who was buried the 29th day of March 1682".*

From his father Thomas Butlin, born December 10th, 1791, William Butlin, the ironmaster of Spratton, Northamptonshire (my great-grandfather) born June 24th, 1824, inherited the ironworks at Wellingborough known as Thomas Butlin and Co.

I have found a number of memorials in Spratton church and churchyard to the Butlin family, including (interior), *"Sacred to the memory of Edward Butlin Esq, born July 20th, 1793; died April 15th, 1878"*. In the churchyard, *"Thomas Butlin, November 29th, 1836. Also Mary, wife of Edward, August 6th, 1861, aged 60. Also eldest daughter of the above, September 9th, 1861 aged 22, Also of Edward, aged 83"*.

William became a wealthy man. He was the first man to smelt iron in the county. Born June 24th, 1824, he married Sarah Clarke, born 1827 (whose parents are buried in the old cemetery at Wellingborough) and they had seven surviving children, of whom my grandmother was one.

No doubt the house at Spratton became too small for the growing family and they moved to Duston House where the children grew up. William's brother Edwin, remained at Spratton and when the children went to visit their uncle he used to call out to his house-keeper to "fill them rough".

The eldest child of William and Sarah was William Henry, born in 1851. He was followed in quick succession by Sarah Ellen (Nellie); George Wallis; Mary Sophia (Sophie, was my grandmother); Thomas Edwin (Tom); Albert; Fanny (died as a child); and Frederick James (Fred) born 1870, nearly 20 years after his eldest brother.

Their father was frequently away on business trips, sometimes abroad. He never came home without bringing toys for the boys and dolls for the girls.

Duston House was given lavish treatment, with conservatory and billiard room. William owned a yacht and joined the Royal Yacht Squadron at Cowes, where he appeared at the annual Regatta. The captain of his crew was a man called de la Rue. When a member of the house party asked on one occasion for a piece of chicken, he was told by a crew member "there was only the drumstick left and Dolly Rue had that".

Going on holiday to Weymouth in 1897 William Butlin died suddenly. He was brought back to Duston and was buried in the churchyard, the first interment in the new family vault. This had not been ready when his son Albert died and he was taken back to Spratton. Over the vault, in recognition of his sailing exploits, was laid a great iron anchor.

Frederick James Butlin, known as F.J.B. was born in January 1870. Like his other brothers he entered the "works". After his father's death he lived with his mother and elder brother William at 39 East Park Parade, Northampton, and after his death with William at the Grove, Tiptree, Essex. After Will's death he moved in 1931 to a nearby village, at the Limes, Kelvedon, Essex where he died in 1954. He remained a bachelor. He was not brought back to the family vault at Duston – though there was room for one more – but cremation was at Ipswich.

The two surviving daughters of William and Sarah Butlin both married doctors on the staff at Berrywood Asylum, Duston.

The elder daughter and second child, Sarah Ellen (Nellie) married Dr. George Millson, who was Medical Superintendent at Berrywood. She died in 1925 and he died in 1938 when he was, I believe, 98. They had two daughters, Ethel, who married Richard Turner, and Nina, also a son, Edgar, who was killed in the 1914–18 war. In their old age the two daughters lived at 63 St. George's Avenue, Northampton.

Second daughter and fourth child of William and Sarah, Mary Sophia Butlin, my grandmother, was born on May, 28th 1854, at Spratton, but brought up at Duston House. She married at Duston Parish Church on August 14th, 1879, Dr. John Ireland Bowes, of Elham, Kent, assistant medical officer at Berrywood Asylum. In 1881 he was appointed medical superintendent at the Wiltshire County Lunatic Asylum (now Roundway Hospital) at Devizes, retiring in 1914. He died in 1929 and she in 1946, aged 91. They had two sons and a daughter, my mother. The Butlin sons either remained bachelors or had only daughters; only the Butlin daughters had sons and this line of Butlin died out with Fred's death in 1954.

Some of William Butlin the ironmaster's descendents may be gleaned (upon the entries in a bible dated 1719).

William Butlin born September 15th, 1761; Sarah Butlin (his wife) born April 25th, 1761; *Thomas Butlin* (founder of the ironworks) born December 10th, 1791; Edward Butlin born July 20th 1793; Mary Butlin, born August 26th, 1795; Harriett Butlin born May 28th, 1798; Sarah Butlin, born February 8th, 1800; Hannah Butlin born April 1780; Eleanor Butlin (wife of Thomas Butlin) born May 12th, 1795; Mary Butlin born March 7th, 1816; Sarah Ellen Butlin born August 1st, 1820;

William Butlin (the ironmaster, son of Thomas and Eleanor) born June 24th, 1824; Sophia Butlin (daughter of Thomas and Eleanor Butlin) born June 20th, 1828; Edwin Butlin (son of Thomas and Eleanor Butlin) born May 16th, 1833.

I don't know where this bible (a Burkitt Bible) now is, but I understand that the first three entries were in very faded ink. The last six were all in the same handwriting probably Williams.

One of William's sisters married a man called Docker. One of their two sons, Alfred was head of a firm of solicitors in Golders Green called, Docker Andrews. He died about 1932, but the firm was still in existence comparatively recently.

Sarah Butlin or Grandma Butlin as she was widely known, moved to 39, East Park Parade, Northampton, where she lived with her eldest and youngest bachelor sons, William and Fred. She died there on March 29th, 1918, when she was a short way off 92. In her executors account is the line, "mourning for servants £8", she was buried in the family vault.

All the sons of William and Sarah Butlin went into the works, but Wallis broke away and set up on his own in the north country.

The eldest son, William Henry, or Sir William Butlin as he became, was born on April 26th, 1851. He studied metallurgy at Cambridge University and iron smelting at Wellingborough, eventually becoming chairman and managing director of his father's firm T. Butlin & Co. Ltd., a position he held for 24 years. He was Spanish Vice-Consul for Northampton and was awarded the Cross of Isabel La Catolica, of Spain. He published a book *Evolution on Revolution,* over the name Ironicus. In *Who's Who* his hobbies are listed as; "Reading, writing, antiques, walking, boating, travel, billiards, etc.". He remained a bachelor. He was knighted in 1921 for services to Spain. On his meetings with other ironmasters he used to come across a young man with a pipe. His name was Stanley Baldwin and he "was always talking politics".

On his mother's death in 1918 Will made a home with his youngest brother Fred, at the Grove, Tiptree, Essex.

Sir William was on a visit to the Channel Islands in 1923, when on May 13th he dropped down dead while dressing in his hotel bedroom. His body was brought back in a triple coffin for burial at Duston. This last interment in the family vault was the last big gathering of the Butlin clan. The Butlins never wished to travel from Duston because of the expense involved in bringing them to the family vault and it is ironic that William Butlin, the father, should have died at Weymouth, and his eldest son, Sir William, in the Channel Islands.

Second son and timid child of William and Sarah Butlin was Benge Wallis Butlin, known by his second name. He launched out on his own and settled in Leeds as an engineer. He married first Laura Humble a Yorkshire girl and when she died young, he fell in love with her sister Alice. By English law at that time he was unable to marry his deceased wife's sister, so he took her to the Channel Islands and married her their. When Parliament later put through the Deceased Wife's Sister Bill, they went through a form of marriage again. Wallis died in 1936 and Alice in 1949. There were no children.

Third son and fifth child of William and Sarah was Thomas Butlin. He married Ethel Knight. They had one daughter Joyce Phoebe, who married Stanley Dodwell, a China Tea planter. They had two daughters and a son who died in a Japanese prisoner of war camp.

Fourth son and sixth child of William and Sarah Albert died a young man. At "the works" one day he dropped down dead at the feet of his brother Fred.

HALL CLOSE

Hall Close stood off Millway (now Sussex Close) with 4 acres of formal gardens, with its superbly kept drive, a lovely golden privet hedge, croquet lawns and fine specimen trees, holly, copper beech still grace the walk from Millway to the "Melbourne Arms". A grand orchard of five to six acres was the other side of the walk. Mr. Matthewson built this fine house completing it in 1914. When he died in 1963 the property was demolished and redeveloped. Now this site was supposed to have been the site of the manor house and for the misdeeds of the Coke family (the builders of Melbourne Hall in Derbyshire) legend has it that for their loyalist tendencies this building was destroyed in the civil war, although there is no record, we do know that the old Millway Cottages were originally known as Manor Cottages, we do know that the oldest parts of the village were South of the old Norman church, and also in its day was in a very commanding position overlooking the upper Nene Valley.

We know that stone floor tiles have been dug up in the cottage gardens over the years, and Mrs. House, daughter of Mr. Matthewson said for fifty years repeatedly that visitors and the family would find white figures or strangers appear in front of them or walking in the garden.

The following comes from a book entitled "Mid Rival Roses" by H.O.M. (from Ray Lagdons earlier History of Duston).

On the summit of the northern assent sloping up the valley of the Nene, the ancient Manor House reared it's crenellated walls. Built by the second Peveril in the time of Reus (King William the Second 1087–1100 and who succeeded the Conqueror on the throne.) Upon a yet older foundation and added to by its late possessors, instrumental in its irregular out lines of tower and turret, pinnacle and bastion gargoyles and gables a conglomerate of castle and mansion. The moat once surrounded it and in the course of time it had grown dry, and somber yew trees dark and gloomy. There was something in the exterior of the edifice that made it a fitting, brooding place for the spirit of violence and evil deeds. The interior corresponded with the external character, dark vaulted passages and winding stone staircase connected the low ceiling black oak panelled cambers. Below huge cellars capable of serving on occasion the purpose of dungeon and stores. In the lofty banqueting hall and the chapel the sun in its zenith could only cast a dim and ghostly light through the deep embrasures where half opaque panes were still further obscured by the blazons of Peveril, Wakelin and DeGray.

1. POND HOUSE, HARRIS BROWN

Henry Harris Brown was the son of Henry Brown, a bookseller and stationer in Gold St. Northampton where he was born in 1864. As he grew up he became absorbed in books and art. His father sent him to the old Northampton Art School where he excelled in sketches and paintings. Later he was encouraged to become a professional painter and went to London and Paris to complete his education. He soon became qualified as one of the leading portrait painters in the country. At 32 years old he had his first pictures accepted by the National Academy. His fame eventually led him to commissions around the world painting wealthy celebrities of his time and nobility, also commissions for magazines in this country and abroad. For many years exhibited at the Salon of the Societe National des Beaux-Arts, Paris and in 1902 the French Government purchased his portrait, Mrs. Boyd of Glastry, for the National Collection at the Luxembourg Gallery; his portrait of William Alexander, Archbishop of Armagh, was purchased for the National Gallery of Ireland; and his picture of Mrs. Hungerford Pollen is included in the Winthrop Collection in the Fogg Museum, Harvard University exhibited Mrs. Arthur Dugdale at the Societe des Artistes Francais 1908 (Mention Honourable); and Mrs. Ince Anderton, 1911 (medal); member of Royal Society of Portrait Painters; he has painted many portraits in the United States and in Canada. Northampton art exhibitions were graced with his studies of still life and children at play. With Mr. G.H. Stevenson the Duston Architect they designed Pond House he never resided there for any length of time owing to his continued business commitments so he installed his parents there in their retirement and both are still remembered by some Duston residents. Local specimens of his art are the portraits of Sir Henry Randall in his mayoral robes and Sir James Barry in Northampton Town Hall. He never married and lived to 83 years old. All his life he loved gardening and his London house and studios were Garden House, 20 the Vale, Chelsea.

2. POND HOUSE, MR. E.G. ELLIOTT

When Mr. E.G. Elliott came to live at Pond House in 1936 he began his career in the boot and shoe trade in the offices of Messrs Manfield and Sons Ltd. but he left to join the old firm of J. Sears the founder to True Form Boot Co., he quickly rose to be company secretary in the late 1930's this was a huge concern owning 270 retail shops he later became a director then managing director with Mr. Dudley Church. He died at the age of 57 shortly after leaving Pond House to prepare for his retirement in another house at Moulton. His first wife Gertrude Glady's died at Pond House and is buried in Duston Churchyard.

3. POND HOUSE, MISS BOUVERIE

In 1940 Delapre Abbey the home of the Bouverie's for 200 years was requisitioned by the War Office and Mrs. Bouverie moved to Pond House. Tragically she was bedridden nearly all her stay at Duston, she was the last person to occupy the House at Delapre. After the War the house was in such a bad state that plans were made to demolish it, but for the efforts of the late Miss Joan Wake it was saved and served for some 40 years as Northamptonshire Record Office, so ill she became that her wish was to die in her old home that arrangements were made by her agent Mr. Ansell to return. As the Abbey was still occupied alterations were made to turn part of the old stable block into a flat, horse standings were taken out and rooms were made beneath what was the coachmans bothy, it was here that she died. Her last Journey was made across the fields to Hardingstone Church, where the coffin was laid on a farm wagon pulled by a pair of shire horses.

4. MORAY LODGE

Was built by Rev. Rodney Granville Randolph in 1904, the first property to be built in what is now Peveril Road, and for some years remained Randolph Road before more houses were built. He retired from his living at St. Kyn and Willin at Newport Pagnell, Bucks. He was educated at Christ Church Oxford and ordained in 1876. He came from a distinguished family, his father Admiral Sir George Granville Randolph fought in the Crimea War. His funeral took place in Duston on July 30th, 1927, conducted by the Rev. E.R. Jones. In his retirement a licensed preacher for Duston and the diocese, for many years now this house has been a home for the elderly.

OAK LODGE, DUSTON

"Oak Lodge" in Old Duston is a delightful example of late 19th century private housing, built entirely of local Duston stone. Mr. George Henry Stevenson, one of Northampton's famous architects built this house for himself in the village, trained by Matthew Holding, he later was in partnership with J.W. Dorman and together carried out many important commissions in Northampton. By 1895 he continued his own practice. There are some outstanding examples of his work especially in local stone. Some examples are the Cock Hotel, Weston Favell House, built for W.J. Sears, Dr. Shipmans house on the roundabout at Bants Lane and many others in this highly residential area for business men at that time. Now most of these are sheltered accommodation of some kind. He also designed new private housing estates around Northampton including Bouverie Estate, Far Cotton, were designed from his original plans also Ashwood Road, Beechwood Road in Old Duston were spoken of as Stevensons Estates.

He served on the first Parish Church Council here after 30 years of service to Duston Church, in 1897 he designed new oak clergy desks and seats and a new stone pulpit (alas the pulpit has gone) and was instrumental on a committee of erecting the War Memorial and vesting it in the care of the Parish Council in 1921. He was born here and laid to rest in the churchyard in 1928.

Public Houses

THE MELBOURNE ARMS, Old Duston

Names after the second Lord Melbourne, Queen Victoria's first Prime Minister as was Melbourne Gardens and Melbourne Lane (now Franklins Gardens) dates from around this time. In 1849 William Hollowell was the victualler and maltster, by the latter part of the 19th century all the land was in a depressed state, corn was coming from the new world in ever increasing quantities, men were leaving the land and whole families went from this area to Manitoba in Canada. Every Lady Day the Lord of the Manor met his tenant farmers with his agent in the Melbourne Arms, one at a time in a private room to talk about the years farming and to collect rent. A farmers daughter some 20 years ago (she was then almost 80) talked about her father meeting Lord Walter Kerr (who eventually sold the estate) and cap in hand saying how sorry he was, but he again had no rent to give, the reply was, "Carry on trying and pay some next year." There would be no applicants for the tenancy if he was to try to relet the farm.

Around this time Quoits was a popular game in this area played in the yard of the Melbourne Arms. Many years ago at Harlestone, I remember seeing a huge silver bowl with small shields around it commemorating the various winners. Harlestone's "Fox and Hounds" were the last winners of the trophy, winning and retaining it after the last competition which was before the first world war.

THE FORGE HAMMER, Old Duston (St. James)

Built with the first part of Alma Street in 1878 it helped to quench the thirsts of Stensons Foundry workers, but drink was also fetched by boys for the ironstone workers in the Weedon Road pits as the building was on the edge of the six fields (six fields to Duston Mill), it was also used by furnace workers from Hunsbury Hill returning after a 12 hour shift across the fields to St. James.

THE FLORENCE, Old Duston (St. James)

The Florence Nightingale was a shoeworkers pub in Devonshire Street, known in my young days as "Hells Kitchen". I remember the old gas lamps, the heavy laden smokey atmosphere, the bar with its sawdust spittoon all the way around. The bar was demolished in the 1950's along with Alma Street to make way for the present blocks of flats.

THE TRAM CAR, Old Duston (St. James)

In the Old Duston parish down St. James square vicinity every street had a pub, this seemed to be the order of the day. In 1878 the old Spencers land the other side of the road was the "Foundry Arms" now the "Foundrymans Arms". Mr. Tipping landlord in the 1930's was a great fisherman and so he attracted many local followers to the sport when he kept the old "Tram Car". So that many passengers coming back from town would ask for a ticket to the Tram Car although St. James would be on the front of the tram. Many years ago St. James End was the hamlet around Mill Road, later the term was used for the whole of St. James.

THE QUARRY ARMS, NEW DUSTON

When New Duston employed large numbers of men in all the stone pits towards the end of the last century, another public house was built at the end of the stone houses of Quarry Road (now the Post Office), it only operated a few years as the demand for Port Road stone declined.

THE WOODEN SPOUT, Old Duston

Not far from the present vicarage, was the old village schoolmasters house. Today it has a plaque on the entrance to show the past occupant. This was a public house in Victorian times and derived a lot of its custom from the extensive iron ore extraction in the Mill Way area.

THE RIFLE BUTT, NEW DUSTON

The Rifle Butt at New Duston shows a Mr. Smith there in 1866, Maltster, Harriet Smith his daughter succeeded him. The Smith family is remembered by Dick Coleman, 88 now living in Port Road. Large gardens or a good range of farm buildings, he said were in the area, now a car park. Dick was born in the old "Hare & Hounds" public house opposite the "Rifle Butt", it was always "The Coleman House" situated in the Harlestone parish.

THE SQUIRRELS, Old Duston

Dating from the 1840's a Mr. Harrison is shown as the landlord. In 1849 a time when Duston House was built as a Dower House by the Samuel family stood in a large park area with its main entrance from Berrywood Farm Road via a private drive from Upton House. Long before, this part was sold for a Mental Hospital in 1876. Duston House is still adorned with coats of arms of the Samuel family, predominant on each are two red squirrels, so it is thought that the pleasing sandstone property originated as part of this complex.

THE GREEN MAN, Old Duston (St. James)

The Green Man was among the *17th Century Inns* published in the *History of Records of Upton Vol. 1*, it was in the old parish of Duston in St. James Road, but a much older building in 1830, in the old records of Duston parish church several inns including the "Green Man" rented pews, I rather think for the family and servants of the publican. In 1849 Charles King is listed as victualler and farmer of St. James (in common with many others at that time). Very little is known about "Harborough Arms" which was built much later, it was a large property pulled down in the late 1930's to widen the entrance of St. James Mill Road.

THE RED HOUSE, Old Duston (St. James)

The Red House now "Red Rover" completely rebuilt in the 1930's replaced a delightful wayside house in my young days with long wooden forms outside for the summer, a favourite meeting place for a large number of allotment holders. A very large area of allotments in the close proximity was Windsor Crescent, St. James Working Mens Club, Weedon Road, Georges Close (Ellesmere Ave. area), Franklins Crescent field etc. I remember as a boy Jimmy Ayres having a small holding near Mill Lane, an old Boar War veteran. He hawked his vegetables and fruit with his horse and cart till in his seventies in St. James calling at one public house after another for ales and refreshment. One Saturday morning having almost completed his rounds I stopped him as he was coming out of the Forge Hammer in Alma Street and asked him if he could give me a lift to my fathers nursery in Mill Lane, soon after climbing on and sitting next to him he was fast asleep, the horse slowly taking him home. There, his gate was open and not until the horse stopped inside did he wake up. As I got down from the cart I said, "Mr. Ayres I thought your last call was at the "Red House". "Well", he said, "the old horse noticed the doors were shut as it had gone closing time (2.00 p.m.) so he kept going".

1908

Henry Harris Brown, photographed with his parents outside their home Pond House, Old Duston.

1867

William Butlin, who then lived in Duston House, went every day to his Wellingborough Iron Works, he also at one time owned Hunsbury Hill Furnaces.

1920

Matthewson's House, Millway

Duston Iron Ore Pits

Duston Iron Ore Pits Commercial extraction of Iron ore in this Duston Parish began in 1854 but it is thought the ore was used here by the Romans on account of the used slag found here a century ago. The demand was not always commercially viable, for the ore and more than one company failed. John Carter Lucas leased the 30 acres of Glebe Land on the North of the Weedon Road and also opened up opposite land on the south side and built a rail terminus for servicing the rolling stock there. This full gauge line connected the old Peterborough line also supplied bricks coal etc. to a large wharf down St. James skirting Franklins Gardens the track went across the first two meadow fields at the bottom of Abbey Street to Lincoln Road also supplying Stenson Iron Works. At Duston Mill the flood plain of the Upper nene was crossed by a heavy timber structure built in a half circle curvature to withstand the heavy water pressure at flood time. Also provision was made for the trucks to empty ore in the barges at Duston Canal Wharf. Lady Palmerston who came into possession of the Duston estate from her brother 2nd Lord Melbourne who died in 1848. At her death Lord Palmerston as Lord of the manor opened the railroad in 1854. Most of the land adjacent to the Weedon Road was hand dug to a depth of 40ft with very little overburden to be taken off. This was wheeled on iron wheelbarrows, across planks on high derricks where they were exposing the iron ore on to the site already mined, this top soil replaced on to subsoil, was endless piece work for the men and very dangerous especially on long planks that would bounce up and down as they went along, they said as they walked the plank so each step was made as the plank bounced up not down. The Mineral agent who lived in Duston for 60 years was responsible for seeing that the land taken of the tenant farmers was levelled off, hedges replanted and a strict system of lease to the Iron Ore Company whereby each half year a portion of the fields were extracted according to a set plan. It also was his task to see his workmen were encouraged and rewards to hand in any finds they made even a pint of beer, was a penny. Two tunnels connecting the workings either side of the Weedon Road were built between 1854 and 1900 and a few years ago it was interesting to again go under one of them. Some 40ft of refuse had to be removed before the part of the intersection (Upton Way, Tolegate, and Weedon Road) could be built. (It is interesting to note that from the the 1920s until mid 1970s raw refuse was tipped on practically all the mined land, hence the building problems of today in this area.

After the death of Lord Palmerston with no direct heir in 1869 all the estates of the late Lord Melbourne passed to Earl Cowper whose vast estates were in Hertfordshire he was the son of Lady Palmerston by her first marriage to the fifth Earl Cowper of Althorpe. He died without issue and his sister Annabel Kerr added more estates to this already very wealthy family Admiral Lord Walter Kerr added still more estates to this already very wealthy family Admiral Lord Walter Kerr her heir decided in 1919 to dispose of a lot of the estates, and so Duston was sold off. He is remembered in my letters from Mr. Bailey.

Various companies continued to extract ore in this area under the name of Duston Iron Ore Company at one time a large quantity of bricks were produced at the Weedon Road supply depot, underneath the great depth of ore was deep blue clay, the pit I remember off Brickyard Lane now Ross Way was full of water in the 1920s and the "stink was awful with raw refuse, the paper etc. blown over a wide area. Mr. Bailey in his letters describes the closure of these pits and the men who worked hard for a £1 a week would not go back on the land for 12/- so they emigrated mostly to Ontario in Canada. At this Duston sale, all tenants were offered their properties to workers, cottage £50 a 300 acre farm with buildings £700, public house, the Mill etc. were all offered to sitting tenants. A grand auction sale of the remaining 1,045 acres and property surplus to the private sales was begun on the 3rd July 1919. So ended the private ownership, 250 years of the Melbourne, Palmerstone, Cowper, Kerr, families who owned the Duston Estate.

Report of the opening of the Duston Iron Ore Line
Duston Iron Ore Company

from "Northampton Mercury" 10th June 1884

"On Monday 8th June 1884, the ceremony of opening the works at Duston, Northamptonshire, took place. The directors, accompanied by several of the principal shareholders, left the Euston station at an early hour and upon arrival at Northampton were met by the Rev. Mr. Cox, the rector of Duston and part proprietor of the property. Lord Palmerston, the other proprietor, was prevented attending through his ministerial duties, but sent a communication congratulating the directors upon the progress they had made. The company, after inspecting the various work, were drawn along the railway constructed for conveying the ore and bricks to the Northampton and Peterborough line. Upon arriving at the end of it, Mr. Bisgood, the chairman, addressed the assemblage at some length, and declared the works opened. The railway constructed by the company is of a most substantial description, one mile in length, passing by a viaduct over the River Nene. A branch is then made to the Grand Junction Canal, affording the advantages both of water and railway conveyance. The line joins that of the London and North-Western, about a mile and a half from the town of Northampton, and at this point a siding for the company's trucks has been laid down, upwards of a quarter of a mile in length. The company afterwards proceeded to the George Inn, Northampton, where an excellent dinner was provided. Mr. Bisgood, who presided, after giving the usual toasts, gave healths of Lord and Lady Palmerston, and referred to the very liberal manner in which his lordship had acted towards the company. A similar compliment was also paid to the Rev. Mr. Cox and Mr. Rivolta, box to Mr. Lucas, the managing director. The whole of the proceedings appeared to give great satisfaction to all present. It may be started that the ore is scarcely three feet from the surface, containing from 40 to 60 per cent, of iron and is from 20 to 30 feet deep. The works require no shaft, as it is merely cutting down a hill. The proprietors also anticipate a profitable return from their brickmaking operations."

In 1854 an agreement was made with Lord Palmerston and John Carter Lucas and Thomas Lucas for the extraction of ore similar to an earlier one in 1850 under the direction of Frederick James, Viscount Melbourne.

"Lessees to perform all the covenants entered into by the late Frederick James Viscount Melbourne with Messieurs Bouverie in a lease dated the twenty fifth day of September, One Thousand eight hundred and fifty two, save that the lessors are to pay the rent under such lease and lessees are to pay lessors twenty five pounds per Annum in lieu of paying such rent and for the benefit of such lease and if required lessees to have an Underlease of said premises demised by said lease of twenty fifth September One Thousand Eight Hundred and Fifty Two."

"Lessees to erect Furnaces within twelve months to be capable of smelting of manufacturing not less than Two Hundred Tons of Pig Iron per week with suitable blowing or blast engineer engines and all other smelting furnaces shall be erected on a spot to be forthwith agreed upon between the parties hereto."

Tenants to have power to get clay and make bricks and tiles sold off the land on Royalty of 2/- per 1,000 such rent to be payable on the twenty fifth of March every year.

Lessors to have the option at the end of the intended lease of taking a valuation all or any of the Bridges Erection Rail or Tramways made by Leysees but all cart roads or earthwork is to be left without payment, the main line of Rail or Tramway to be decided upon between the parties and counterpart and to have power to determine said lease at any time on giving three calendar months notice.

Lessees to have power to work such part of the Limestone under the Lands in the Plan marked as may be agreed upon paying sixpence for every lot of two thousand four hundred of the raw stone raised and used upon the Estate and One shilling for every such lot sold off the Estate wither in the raw state or made into lime for the purpose of sale and to work the Limestone in the workman like manner as regard the depth and without waste of usable or marketable Limestone

Lessors reserve all other minerals save Ironstone and in the event of their intention to demise or get them lessees to have the first offer to take them upon fair and equitable terms.

Duston Iron Ore Pits

Memorandum of Agreement made and entered into this First day of July One thousand eight hundred and fifty four Between The Right Honourable Henry John Viscount Palmerston and Emily Mary Viscountess Palmerston his Wife of the one part and John Carter Lucas and Thomas Lucas of 113 Aldersgate in the City of London Drysalt Thomas Wolley of 15 Frenchchurch Street in the City of London Ship broker, Thomas Baker of 36 Newgate Street in the City of London Esquire and Robert Beevor of Saint Lawrence Ramsgate in the County of Kent, Esquire of the part as follows:

Lease to be granted for Thirty Years from Lady Day One Thousand eight hundred and fifty four off all the Ironstone in the fields marked in the plan amend situate in the Parish of Duston Northamptonshire such leave to contain all Covenants clauses provision and agreements as are usual in Mineral Leases and particularly clauses to the following effect.

Lessees to pay a Royalty of Nine pence per Lot or Ton or Two thousand four hundred pounds of Raw Ironstone raised.

To work the Ironstone in a Workman like manner and particularly as regards the depth and all other points and without and waste of the marketable Ore and so as to disturb as little as profitable the agricultural use of the land and to calcine the Ironstone if calcined within One hundred yards of the furnaces.

The minimum Rent for the Ironstone to be Four hundred pounds per Annum for the first three years and Six Hundred pounds a year afterwards payable half yearly but the first half year's Rent is to be payable at Lady Day net Leysees to be allowed a Four years average clause to make up deficiency (if any).

A joint measurement of the workings to be taken half yearly and working plans kept on the premises for inspection of Landlords and their agents with liberty for their principal agent to take copies or extracts.

Leysees to do as little damage as possible to lands or crops and to make compensation to all tenants for such damage done a fair valuation and make good all fences damaged or destroyed and restore when required by Leysees or their agent.

Lessees to make roads Railways or Tramways Foot Roads and other ways for getting the ore and for the convenience of their workmen and also to erect weighing machines on the Leysees land in places to be selected by the said Leysees and approved by the said Leysees.

Leysors their agents servants and other tenants to have power at all time to crop over or under all roads Railways Tram or other ways to be made by Leysees over the Glebe Land or any other adjoining and to use the same and the Wharf Ways to connected therein paying to the Leysees a reasonable compensation for so doing. Leysees to make communications between fields, erect gates to where communication is cut off by any road made by them to make waterways.

By 1863 Messrs Bevan & Co were the second Iron Ore Co. operating, then we find by 1880 Higgins & Co. 1885 an agreement regarding the use of the Duston Iron Ore Co.

Little is known of George Pell who was extracting and burning lime on what is now British Timken site and later the line was used to convey lime to Hunsbury Hill Furnaces, a tramway was used to the full gauge line near the south east side of Duston Church.

William Bailey

I corresponded with the late Bill Bailey for many years he never forgot his friends and relations in the Old Duston Parish where he grew up in one of the worst agricultural depressions at the turn of the century, farmers and their workforce went in large numbers to Canada and most of them found a life in Manitoba and Ontario. Towards the end of his life he was in a position to return having his own son William to look after the farm. Here is his story as he has written it, many years ago. He first mentions the clay pits 40 ft deep later filled with refuse now part of Weedon Road Industrial site off Ross Way. I found one original brick made there many years ago which has in the frog (centre) D.I.ORE.C. (Duston Iron Ore Company). He goes on to recall the full gauge Iron Ore Line from the Peterborough-Blisworth railway to Duston and a further branch to St. James.

1. Brick making took place my time. There was a huge clay pit approx 300 yard from the Ironstone sheds and when I first saw it in 1905 it was full of water. It was almost ground level the meadow end, at the end towards the Weedon Road the ground level was quite high, at least 20 feet with a gradual slope to the other end.There was a good pathway around the water, I often saw men fishing there. Apart from brick dust and chips there was nothing else to be seen at that time.
2. The operations in the Lime stone quarry had ended before my time too, I would say that operations shut down between 1880-1890. When I started to work with the Steaverley Coal and Iron Co. at their Duston branch there wasn't any signs of the narrow gauge line. All traces of it had been removed except the stables where used to keep the horses for hauling on the narrow line.
3. The line from the Ironstone quarries was carried over the meadows, on a bridge or viaduct built with heavy timbers, it started near the river's edge and there was a slight bend to bring it straight on line, with a bridge over the Canal and then to the railway siding going down on the Blisworth side of the roadway over the line. The line was brought to the river's edge on an embankment, I think that is still there. It was quite interesting going to and from the meadows when flooded on the Loco pulling 6 to 10 railway trucks loaded and bringing back a string of empties. The other line to St. James End was disused when I joined the Co. There was part of the line down the meadow but it appeared the St. James End part had been lifted. If I was there I think I could point out where that line went partway down the meadow.

4. Re the stone coffin, at the time, I didn't know what it was. Some evenings on the way home from work I would dally in the pit looking for Roman money and where there was a good depth of black soil I would scratch about and hoping a coin would show up. I did find one good one and three second rate ones and I still have a fair number of pottery fragments. When I was scratching one evening a stone showed up, it was only a stone as far as I was concerned. The workers next day unearthed the coffin. Coins, Urn's or anything of value had to go to the Lord of the Manor and many items are to be seen in the Northampton Museum. The workers got a little extra cash for their items.

5. I do not remember seeing Lord Cooper, Sir Walter Kerr, yes. He was looking over the Duston estates and we had him on the footplate of the loco and took him on a tour of the Ironstone workings and rail. He was over six feet tall and well built and I felt more like a dwarf by his side. At that time there was a dispute on between the Co. and the estate over the royalties. The Co. were paying a shilling a ton and they wanted it reduced to sixpence, that's what they were paying at Cranfords at Loddington. To extend the workings and rebuild the bridge on viaduct over the meadow meant a big expense to the Co. While the discussions were going on, all operations ceased for several months and all the staff except the Foreman and the Loco drivers were transferred to Loddington. We used to go by train on Monday morning to Lamport, then it was a long walk to the Ironstone workings across the fields, we returned to Northampton on Saturday mornings. The Duston operations started again and one day orders came through to pack up and after some of the track had been lifted and some ground somewhat levelled, the estate offered to take the sipence a ton. Alas it was too late and the packing up continued and completed in the early months of 1909. My childhood days were spent in Millway, at the farm at Berrywood, and the last 7 years at Duston School, I didn't miss a day or was late either.

1969

Old iron stone bank across Millway up Millway Fields, here limestone was loaded onto railway wagons from a tramway crossing at Bants Lane and taken to Hunsbury Hill Furnaces.

Old iron ore engine sheds that stood off Ross Way, Weedon Road.

1972

Excavating the old iron ore bank for use on new Tollgate Road.

No: 843 CERTIFICATE OF COMPLETE REGISTRATION.

of the *Duston Iron Ore Company.*

Pursuant to the Act 7 & 8 Vict., c. 110.

I, FRANCIS WHITMARSH, ESQUIRE, *Registrar of Joint* Stock Companies, *do hereby Certify that the* Duston Iron Ore Company is COMPLETELY *Registered according to Law.*

Given under my Hand, and Sealed with my Seal of Office, this eleventh *day of* September *Eighteen Hundred and Fifty* Four

George Taylor

Assistant *Registrar of Joint Stock Companies.*

1854

Registration of the first iron ore company in Duston.

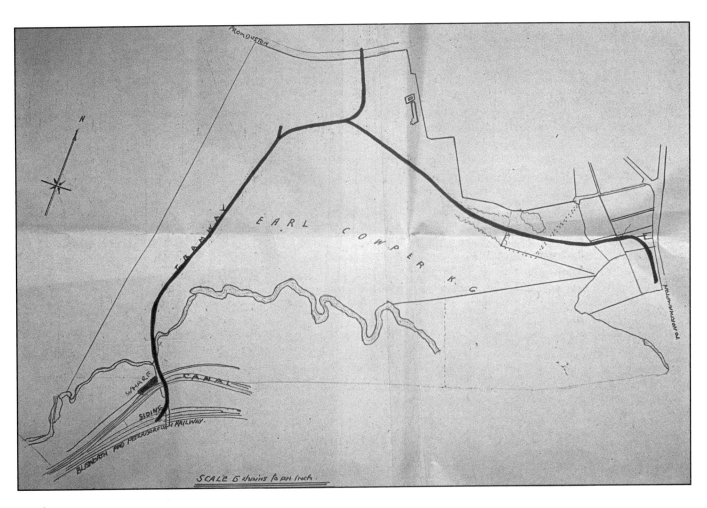

1876

Earl Cowper's iron ore line from Duston sidings to St. James and the two links to Duston ore fields.

1900

Iron Ore workers showing overhead walkway to remove the overburden (topsoil).

Duston Nurseries

This old Mill Lane nursery site for some 40 years a growing flower nursery except during the last war when the sixteen acres was put down to vegetables. This 8 acres of ours confronting the Weedon Road was always wanted for raw refuse filling, the borough of Northampton tipped on some 100 acres of old ironstone land from 1920 to 1980. In the early days of tipping the neighbouring smells were intolerable, so much so that Weedon Road was a no go area for years, before and after the war, all hedges were covered with waste paper and rubbish, rats galore, it wasn't until the last few years of tipping that sufficient amounts of rat poison were put down in areas close to the tipping that this menace was finally controlled, the spraying of winged insects, crickets ect. that we finally came to controlled tipping.

The nearer the ironstone excavation sites came within close proximity of Duston Church, so early settlements were exposed, Iron Age, Saxon, Norman, all south of the church to the Weedon Road. It is interesting that the Church Way does not come from a Main Road entrance, but comes from the ancient village area in Millway. An environment archaeologist, Samuel Sharpe who lived at Dallington Hall in the latter part of the 19th Century, was in charge of all this historic area findings in co-operations with the Lord of the Manors mineral agent Mr. Garrett. All the Iron workers were encouraged to hand in all finds and were rewarded with a penny or even two, which would buy a pint or two of beer.

As a boy, with my fathers old workers some of these came to work long after the Quarries finished and I loved to hear them talk of their days working. In the late 20s they were about the same in their old corduroys always strung up at the knees (untied after work) so their bottoms of their trousers were kept clean. As I have already mentioned, in their quarrying days they loved to come back on a site, to look into the fresh exposed banks of ore and look for signs of past disturbance of soil that would lead them to a "find". In a busy working day such finds could be overlooked, and the rewards were well worth having around. The old nursery site was part of the largest Roman site in the county and produced 100s of artifacts, they remembered the burial site where the limestone tomb was found the Roman well etc. in the iron ore extraction. The tomb now stands on the ground floor of the Abington Museum and must weigh several tons.

Mill Lane nursery was dug 40 feet deep by hand in the late latter part of the 19th century. As boys we had to climb up a forty rung ladder up the side of pit banks to ferret rabbits. After the ore was extracted the over burden was barrowed back and then topsoiled to enable the fields to be productive again. In my youth it was interesting to be taken to the old pit. Workers who in their declining years would come and spend a summer working for my father. They then for this midday meal would sit under a hedge and have the top of a cottage loaf, a piece of cheese perched on top, an onion pressed down firmly with the thumb. In the left hand the well worn sheffield pocket knife, slicing off each portion as required and washing down with cold tea from a bottle with no sugar or milk.

As the digging of the ironstone moved from the lower part of the Weedon Road to the Millway crossroads, through the tunnels, a pathway was made in a straight line north to the village, and every six months the mineral estate agent pegged out a section for the iron ore company from the opening of the tunnel mouth anticlockwise so that the rail track followed the extraction round in 45% circle to complete that area. Men wheeled the topsoil and overburden on twenty feet planks on top of 30-40 feet high derricks down onto the new level. Their iron wheelbarrow with nearly 3 cwt in, each day cut deep groves in the 14" heavy planks. It was almost a circus act to wheel them along those barrowing planks. The old workers told me you had to put down your foot as the bouncing planks come up. For some 60 years the Borough of Northampton tipped raw refuse on all the extraction land except ours and now a larger part of the filled in area is industrial and on the southside the Nene Valley had its problems with methane gas.

Life on the old nurseries

When father started his Millway Nurseries after the first would war he could not afford much labour so a lot of seasonal work was done by pensioners eager to supplement their existence by a few shillings. They were hardy strong men often in their seventies, eager to talk about the bad old days of the 1880's off to the Boer War working hours nearly 12 hours a day till 4 o'clock Saturdays, holidays, Good Friday and Christmas Day. Then nursery work was spades, hoes and forks all cleaned after work and put away each day, each had their own. They said it was to their hand the hoe blade correct to a certain angle for their height the spade and fork would be preferred to correspond to their hands and movement and often they would be taken to the Duston Blacksmith to be adjusted. Woe betide any young man starting work and found in possession of an old regulars implement. Winter even in the glasshouses was a time for preparing for the coming spring in very severe weather even with a minimal amount of labour every four years soil would be removed to a depth of 2ft for tomato crop replacing fresh soil from outside after manuring, the base taking 1ft off. It was ideal when the outside soil was frozen, with picks we would break it up in large lumps and barrow it in over the frozen ground, if there had been a heavy snowfall, we would bring a good 1 foot of that in as well. This resulted in a huge crop of tomatoes for at least two years (long before steam sterilising was widely used in nurseries). For all glasshouses use, potting compost was soil based, a huge stack of ingredients were carefully arranged in layers like an enormous sandwich, meadow turf, farmyard manure, lime leaf mould ect. were all needed to decompose for a general purpose compost. This stood for a whole year then was cut down and put through a fine sieve as required. Some 30 years later this annual procedure was still in operation but by then steaming the compost before using was operational so was once used clay pots and wooded seed boxes.

Today peat based compost is the norm gone are the days of labour intensive nursery work, gone are the heavy clay pots, the barrowing, heavy manuring the enormous preparation of providing ones own personal prepared multi-use compost. Now all we have to do is to fetch a scientifically prepared colourful bag of carefully prepared formula and carry on potting. But we cannot go back . . . . . . or can we?

The skilled worker with the scythe is no more, shall we hear the rasping sound of the whetstone moving rhythmically. Sharpening each side of the upturned blade was part of the summers day, followed by the swish, swish effortlessly timed cuts was heard across the fields.

If a new scythe was not to his feel and hand he would go to the blacksmith with it and first show the correct measure of his outstretched step for each swathe he would cut then alter the angle of the blade despite the alternate adjustments allowed on the head of the blade.

In those days there were always to be seen a scytheman going to the churchyard to keep the grass tidy, but with his old well worked old bladed scythed to work his way round the gravestones.

Before the introduction of the first lawnmowers all the lawns on the large estate Mansions were cut by hand. One of the men employed by my father in the 1920's did just that, he scythed his own lawn. Coke, once the main source of heating in the old nurseries for almost a century was a labour intensive daily ritual, boilers (ours were the old Robin Hood) morning and evening raking the cinders and ashes out, and during this process one would have to emerge out of the stokehold or gasp fresh air before descending again. As a boy from the age of 13 before midnight in severe winter weather I used to stoke up the boilers at Duston, getting on a carrier bike setting off from Alma Street after lighting the small oil lamp and clamping it on to the side of the front wheel hub. It was essential to leave the dampers open, these were plate in the brick chimneys at ground level to enable the boilers to draw air to boost the firers for late stoking, when the dampers would be pushed in to last till 7.30 a.m. in the morning. So important was this procedure that after returning to bed one bitter night my father opened the bedroom door and said "You made sure the damper was in when you came away,' I said "I think so, well if your not sure you had better go back and make sure."

Not a building of any description was then from the old Duston turn off Weedon Road to the old cross roads at Millway I still remember as a boy that midnight awesome lonely winter ride, down Millway flinging the coke on the boilers and heaving a sigh of relief when I returned to St. James an hour later, I remember my parents walking together three miles in deep snow late at night to do this most essential task of keeping the frost out of the greenhouse. Every summer the coke would be hauled in the nurseries till there was a huge quantity piled up to last for six months. Two loaded drays would leave Foxons yard the railways depot in Andrews Road when they arrived at the bottom of Weedon Road hill the two horses were chained one behind the other to get each load up the hill. After Christmas Mr. Foxon would come to see my father for half the money for the fuel, then Easter the remainder-those were the days. As most Glasshouses were built at that time a section of one of the house was dug out for soft rain water storage as all roof water was saved (No town water arrived in this area until the mid 1930s). This of course was much more beneficial to the plants and used at air temperature, but when the well got low in a hot dry summer the only other source was the river so a horse and cart loaded with barrels made the one mile journey uphill to the nurseries, time after time until the concrete tanks were full, three men (one on the cart) would pass up buckets of water, bad language when one of the inadvertently threw a bucketful over one of them. The workers started their day and finished by the Gas house blower in town, they said it was-among so many-the most reliable to the minute, during the day. The small engine going backwards and forwards on the Blisworth line also informed them of the time during the day, a single coach, two coaches, two pushing and pulling, denoted workmens trains all was part of their day.

1952

Pyrethrums grown for cut flowers on Millway Nurseries.

1959

Wallflowers grown for cut flowers, Hunsbury Hill in the background (no houses whatsoever).

1960

View from Millway of nurseries.

1968

Mill Lane Nurseries, a field of Dahlias.

1975

Millway Nurseries growing Tomatoes for Northampton market.

1956

Bed of Russell Lupins, Millway Nurseries.

1965

Millway Nurseries, a large part of it now Tollgate Way and Sainsbury's.

1936

Mill Lane Nurseries with Mr. John Golby Senior.

1969

Millway Nurseries old type greenhouse of Arum Lilies.

1922

Yardes extensive block of offices and shops newly built, Abington Square.

1947

Yardes sale of old greenhouses
(later British Timken visitors car park site).

THIRD DAY'S SALE.

ON THURSDAY, 4th DECEMBER, 1947,

at 11.30 o'clock.

GREENHOUSES.

No. 1 HOUSE.

LOT
621   A span-roof glasshouse, 60ft. long, 14½ft. wide, 16ft. over, with two glass sides, each 60ft. by 2ft., 2 glass ends and 1 door, with staging to house
622   267ft. run of 4in. hot water piping
623   The brickwork to the house

No. 2 HOUSE.

624   A span-roof glasshouse, 46ft. long, 15ft. wide, 18ft. over, with 2 glass ends and 1 door, and the staging as fitted
625   205ft. run of 4in. hot water piping
626   The brickwork to the house

No. 3 HOUSE.

627   A span-roof glasshouse, 75ft. long, 21ft. wide, 24ft. over, with partition and 2 glass ends and 1 door, with eight lights to propagating frames and the staging and shelving as fitted
628   450ft. run of 4in. hot water piping
629   The brickwork to the house

No. 4 HOUSE.

630   The brickwork (remaining) to this house

631   A 4ft. 6in. Rochford tubular boiler, and piping and connections to outside of Houses Nos. 1, 2 and 3, and supply tank and stoking irons
632   The brickwork to shaft and stokehole

Duston Water Mills

Duston Upper Mill

When William Peveril founded an Abbey for Black Canons for the order of St. Augustine and dedicated it to St. James, he endowed within 40 acres, and the Mill of the parish. Situated on the Upper Nene flood plain, it was more difficult in winter flooding to reach Northampton, than crossing at the South Gate of the town, where the Northern branch met. The Mill continued to grind corn till 1919 when the sale of whole of the Melbourne Duston Estate was sold, its tenant Mr. Thompson did not wish to purchase it, and its new owners only wanted the water meadows for grazing, so its decay began. In 1976 after the whole area was purchased by Northampton Development Corporation for town expansion it was demolished as an unsafe building after strenuous opposition by local people. The Mill House was listed, now that too has also been pulled down. There was also a Water Mill in St. James Abbey one of the references state – Francis Samwell Esq. was Lessee of the Water Mill in Abbots Meadow and late parcel of St. James Abbey.

Duston Lower Mill with a much stronger head of water was a very much larger Mill in its working days (at the end of a long lane). St. James Mill where in the latter part of the last century was also steam powered as were so many larger town Mills. The earliest records of a miller was when it carried the name Perry's Mill. John Daniels we find was there in 1845 and in 1870 was followed by Messrs H. & J.H. Beesley and Sons. Its successors were Northampton Flour Mills Ltd. with F.J. Beesley, a son of the former owners as Secretary, during and after the last war the mill and fields were given over to rearing various breeds of poultry with again the Beesley family, (A.M. and F.J.) partners. By 1956 a Mineral Water Co. had taken over the Mill and property. The area of St. James Lower Mill is now a busy industrial area. The Mill is untraceable and even the Nene water there has been diverted.

1939

Duston Upper Mill.

1965

Mr. Fosdyke, who lived at the Mill House until the demolition of the Mill.

The Cotton family's butchers Sheep St. Shop, Northampton. They bought Duston Upper Mill at the 1919 Estate Sale.

1937

Fishing the Upper Duston Mill

1913

St. James Lower Mill when in use by the Beesley family.

Picture by courtesy of Northamptonshire Libraries.

British Timken

1992 is a memorable year for British Timken. 50 years ago saw the beginning of their manufacturing in Duston beginning a long and fruitful association with Northampton and its county. All I can do is to outline its beginning and growth and importance in regard to Duston now part of the expanding Northampton.

In 1941 the Timken factory at Aston, Birmingham was invited by the Ministry of Supply to find a much safer area away from the bombing and the present site was chosen first on Yardes Nurseries. Tapered roller bearings were first made in this country in 1909 when Vickers Ltd. affected an agreement with the Timken Roller Bearing Co. of America. 1917 the Timken Company became a department of another Vickers group Wolseley Motors Ltd. of Birmingham. 1920 British Timken was formed and became a subsidiary of Wolseley Motors Ltd. 1927 an agreement was made with Timken Roller Bearing Co. to take over British Timken Ltd. 1920 under its chairman Michael Dewar the first tapered roller bearings were being manufactured for British Railways. 1931 the first heavy rolling with bearings were being made. 1939 saw the demand for wartime supplies of Roller Bearings etc. for the Ministry of Supply and the need for a much larger and safer site.

In 1945 Timken employees to celebrate the end of the Second World War, had the idea of holding a works flower show. Little did they realise that from this small show about 4,000 people attended would ultimately command a total of 40,000 people annually making it into one of the finest 2 day shows in the country, sadly now disbanded. This first show was opened in September of that year by the present Earl Spencer's Grandmother with Michael Dewar, Chairman of British Timken and John Pascoe (later Sir John) Managing Director of the present company. The late Leslie Dorricott was the first chairman of the show who together with Mary Finch (now Mrs. Taunton) and the late Bernard Gaffey participated in organising the show for over 25 years and as the show progressed were assisted by an able and loyal committee. 480 entries in the horticultural show of 1945 together with a gymkhana for the children games and relay races, looking at the first schedule for the show the horticultural entries were very small, some 20 acres were later devoted to the show, one of the great attractions being the horse jumping televised annually and famous riders participating. Marquees were provided for local societies own annual shows competing for awards and trophies in bees, rabbits, birds etc. altogether providing a great day for all. The first show raised a total of £350 and given to the late Rev. Dennis Pettit then a curate at St. Luke's responsible for St. Barnabas, New Duston (now demolished) he passed the money on to St. Dunstans as he himself was blinded in the 1914 – 1918 war. He later served as Vicar of Spratton for many years.

Duston has been fortunate in having the generosity of British Timken in funding various buildings and refurbishing others where social activities take place providing amenities connected with local schools and youth activities through the Nene Foundation. The Timken International Fund was originally set up by the grandson of Mr. Henry Timken who founded the Timken company in Canton Ohio U.S.A. continued today by the Timken family, the present Nene Foundation (United Kingdom) branch of Timken International Fund was set up to distribute for charitable purposes in communities. Where British Timken work, people live. Since 1945 £3.2 million has been donated in the Duston and Daventry areas. The Nene Foundation generously gave to the following:

    Community Centre 1974
    Swimming Pool (Upper School)
    St Crispin (work shop) rehabilitation 1970 and 1976
    Upper School grants 1977 and 1991 computer and equipment
    Duston Guides and Brownies (capital sum) 1966
    Millway School Music Room 1983
    Village Institute 1990.

December 15th 1954 saw the memorable visit of the Duke of Edinburgh to Duston to open the running track and lay the foundation stone of the sports pavilion (the late Sir John Pascoe) together with the Mayor Alderman J. V. Collier greeted H.R.H. at the castle station amid cheering crowds. A huge marquee was erected on the showground where H.R.H. took lunch with guests and directors of British Timken. The marquee was beautifully decorated and finished products of the works were on display. After a tour of the factory, the Duke expressed his sincere thanks for his enjoyable visit and a special train awaited his return to London at 4.15 p.m.

1st of April 1978 the new indoor sports centre was opened by Ron Knapp, Managing Director of Timken of Europe (now retired) which the company built for the work force which would offer a much wider range of sports and social activities and possible to seat some 400 members.

Mr Ron Knapp joined British Timken as a graduate apprentice in 1946. After a distinguished service in the Royal Navy Promotions, soon followed from quality control engineer, assistant works manager, chief development engineer. In 1969 he became Managing Director of Timken Europe. 1976 appointed to a director of the Timken Co. Canton Ohio. 1979 received the C.B.E. from the Queen for his services to export. Still living in Duston for over 40 years he now devotes his retirement to his 2 acres of walled garden still enjoying his passion for rugby football after playing for the Saints some 30 years ago.

Part 3 – New Duston

Fossett's Circus

Fossetts Circus is reputed to be the oldest travelling Circus in the British Isles for generations a large part of it has always been at Tiffield where the horses are still trained. At one time after the first war the winter quarters were at Ravensthorpe. In 1919 after the Watkins sale at Hopping Hill the old farm buildings were acquired from Mr. Travis (founder of the Timber Co.). Part of the land was then sold to Mrs. Haddon, a Northampton bookmaker at the time who built a large glasshouse area at the rear of Hopping Hill House. All the remainder of the property was acquired for the Circus over 60 years ago by the circus. This site has now been recently vacated and the present winter quarters are at Milton Malsor. Before the war elephants were exercised in New Duston and many remember Jacob the Indian trainer giving rides to the children. Many years ago I was privileged to visit and see the collection of private old family travelling caravans of Mr. Bailey Fossett. All these old-gaily painted vans were in one of the huge sheds on the site. All have now gone and a few years ago were all shipped to an outdoor Museum in America. They are now completely restored in all their former glory with scores of others. One of their show wagons made in the Seventeenth Century is some 14ft high with lions and figures on top has a geared mechanism which these beautifully painted circus Figures were raised to a height of 17ft. It was drawn by a team of 9 horses pulling some 4 tons in weight and 19ft long. At one time Hopping Hill was an Aladdins cave of old vehicles, I remember seeing old Ford T's several of them and an "Old Horse Tram and the Chariot of "Ben Hur" from the silent film days. Now of course all gone. The late Mr. Bailey Fossett recalls the days of his father at the outbreak of the last war. The circus was on tour at Bala in North Wales and then was immediately returned to Tiffield. Elephants were put to work clearing grounds and pulling up trees to enable the farm to be put to the plough for the war effort. After some time the government allowed the movement of the performing animals to indoor Circuses and Shows for entertainment purposes. Today all these animals are well fed, warm and clean and the Fossett family are is intensely proud of the way all the performing animals are treated.

1950

Part of the old Stable block with the ornate stalls for the performing circus horses at Hopping Hill.

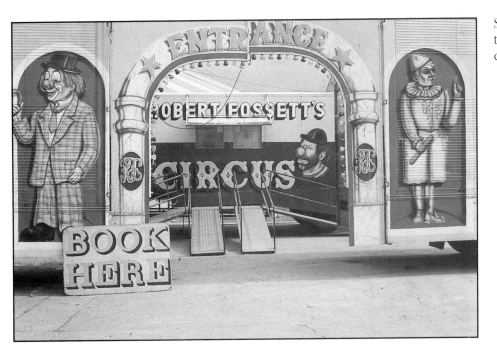

Sir Robert Fossett's Circus on tour set up ready for opening day.

The huge elephant transporter carrying some 36 tons weight from show to show.

1930

Children gathered together at New Duston for a ride on Jacob's elephant from Fossett's Circus.

Duston Eldean School 1950 (First Year)

L-R

Back Row:
   Miss N.E. Kilburn, Judy Shirley, Janet Budge, John Speight, Trevor Goodman, Angela Robinson, Stewart Pearson, Ruth Harrison, Barry Rednall, Ivan Neighbour, Margaret Garrett, Pamela Bonner, Miss K. O' Connor.

Fourth Row:
   Sheila Skitt, Rodney Lewin, Antony Smith, Judith Penn, Carole Perrett, Gwyneth Hughes, Carole Stone, Beryl Strong, Pauline Glasspool, Yvonne Pauline Malin, Sheila Atkinson, Martin Coleman, Colin Grey, Joyce Blundell.

Third Row: Included are
   Christine Jones, Miriam Earp, Malcolm Pearson, Peter Ashby, Shirley Slinn, Tony George, David Husbands, Dane Westley, Janet Garrett, Diane Hawgood, Jennifer Bailey.

Second Row: Included are
   Pamela Clark, Nicholas Patchesa, Jean Lines, Beryl Thompson, David Maycock, Peter Brown, David Piggott, Sandra Mynard, Corrinne Bailey.

Front Row: Included are
   Gordon Meeton, John Lane, Denise Robinson, Margaret Shepherd, Sally Revell, Barry Hobson, Ronald Rogers

1938

New Duston Football Team photographed in "Rifle Butt Yard" (Denton's) personalities present Mr. Handscombe, G. Pendred, Mr. Cockerill, Mr. Cook, Mr. Denton, W. P. Cross.

1936

Jubilee Day with flags flying in Port Road.

1936

King George 5th Silver Jubilee celebrations at New Duston in "Rifle Butt Yard" all the village joined in in this lovely summer's day. Each October the feast of St. Luke's Duston was celebrated with a fair on this site.

1936

Mr. Collins village dairy man in his smart delivery float outside Mr. Blunson's old house. It had Mr. Laxton's general store on the Harlestone Road corner.

1907

In Goldby's old disused stone pits, Port Road. Could the photograph depict Empire Day celebrations

Stone Quarries of Duston

The sandstone of Duston is to be found in all the old buildings in villages around here, together with Harlestone Stone, built most of its Medieval Churches East of Northampton. Indeed around the centre of the old town many of its old historical properties are of the rich brown "Ryland Stone", as are Delapre Abbey, Doddridge Castle Hill Chapel, and The Judges House, Mercers Row. The parish is now built either on sandstone beds or limestone, one has great difficulty in location exactly where the pits were so long ago, all subsequently filled in, and built on since the last war, in this expanding parish. Although huge quantities of sandstone were quarried off the Weedon Road in Victoria times, this contained rich iron ore and could not be dressed or squared for building, but in the New Duston area it was good quality. This busy "stone" hamlet consisted principally of Port Road and Quarry Road built for quarry men and masons. These skilled masons worked in thatched covered stone barns, with a fire place at one end an in each work place a large heavy stone table on which a head stone was placed, some 5 to 3 feet to enable them to do their intricate carving. Large quantities of inferior sandstone called ragstone was used for enclosure walls in the village and in old farm cottages. It is surprising how much poor quality stone was used in some local Church buildings, it is noticeable in additions from the 18th century that much better dressed stone was used.

When Lord Cowper came into the possession of the Duston Estate in 1867 all the buildings were in a very depressed state in stone and thatch. He set about repairing and rebuilding the whole estate, his most notable achievement was the building of the estate houses in Melbourne Lane. These were originally very small barn cottages in pairs (one remained until a few years ago opposite the "Melbourne Arms although now happily converted into one building and modernised). Years ago the occupants climbed up ladder-like stairs to their loftlike bedroom and looked up to rough bark timber and thatch.

Lord Cowper built the new houses from his best quarry stone, they must have seemed like palaces to the tenants, tap water, wash houses and toilets built on, each pair has a datestone and coat of arms to commemorate a generous Lord of the Manor.

In the old days, for alternative roofing stone slate was used as was Collyweston Stone in East Northamptonshire. The parish pit for this was found at the boundary field, New Duston, where Brook Cottage stood, the original stone part of the property began life as slate workers buildings. Over the boundary brook next to the adjoining field was Harlestone slate pits, and some years ago I saw pit workers buildings in the Pheasantry clad with this hard stone, also before Brook Cottage was pulled down the garden paths were edged with the same field slate, Limestone.

Living opposite me in Millway for many years was Stanley Cosford. In his retirement his recollection of his firms achievements in Church building in stone, by his grandfather, working with the celebrated Architect Holding, and later Stevenson. One can find beautiful examples of their combined commissions in Northampton and its County Churches.

His grandfather extracted stone from the estate pits around 1850 to 1860, as tenant of same it enabled him to acquire large quantities of the most suitable quality Ryeland stone. Samuel Goldby took over the stone pits in 1860, he built many fine gentlemens houses in the Harlestone and Dallington area. Many of these properties are a delightful combination of Limestone and dressed Ryeland sandstone, as is the house he built for himself in Port Road with its elegant ornamental porch and datestone S.G. By the early 1930's, Messrs. Martin, the Northampton builders acquired the pits, one of their church commissions was to refurbish All Saints tower with New Duston stone. It is said that when Althorpe Station was built, more Ryland stone was sent away than was ever used locally.

Mr. Blunston's pits were in the area opposite the "Rifle Butt" public house, as far as the small chapel along the Duston Road, across to Harlestone Road, including the site of Orchard Cottages, most of this area is below road level.

Hardly any of this best stone remained in the pits to be extracted by the turn of the century, also the demand diminished on account of bricks being made in huge quantities and cheaper to build with, and the import of Marble and other memorial grave stone, supplied to more and more town funeral masons. The village stone masons were no longer wanted. Eventually the pits were suppliers of ground stone for New Northampton Building Estates. Already the Harlestone Churchyard has been listed as a conservation area in recognition of the work and artistry of its bygone masons.

Generations of these gifted and highly skilled craftsmen have left us with many gravestones to admire in their churchyards, inside their Churches and in their buildings, although our county villages are rich in their local stone, Duston russet brown was the most admired for character and its combination with thatch.

Watkins Pits

Mr. Martin the Northampton builder (also in 1919 Mayor) bought Hopping Hill House for £5,350. The farm (lot 2) was bought by Mr. Travis. The sale catalogue listed Carpenters shop, Paint shop, Blacksmiths shop, Large Dutch barn and Engine house. Also a large Granary, four cottages fronting Harlestone Road, large clay beds providing some of the finest bricks in the county. The works extended from the farm down to what is now Airflow Streamlines, a lot of the original buildings are clad with the lovely red pantiles made there.

In 1890 a Fowler Steam engine No 6141 was used for the site works and for seasonal thrashings and later a more powerful Charles Burre built at Thetford No 1594.

Some years ago I met an angry plumber who had installed small bore pipes for a new heating system in a Watkins house at New Duston, he had to chop all the bricks out instead of boring holes through them as they were so hard. Rupert Watkins who inherited the Watkins Estates and sold them, told me the russett red bricks were baked four times as much as the ones produced in Bedfordshire.

Watkins Bricks

Hopping Hill House which is now Hopping Hill Hotel in the sale catalogue of 1919, was described as having architectural details combining in its decorations, best features of the past and containing ideas well ahead of its time. The residence is constructed of 9" Watkins bricks and faced with 4 1/2" facing bricks with a 2" cavity wall. All the floors carried on 3"x9" pitch pine joists which are plugged in to render the floors noiseless. The fireplaces have unique features of having each hearth furnished with a false flue leading down to the basement, down which flue ashes are brushed, there to be collected. Mr. Watkins personally collected and selected all the oak for the house panelling of the walls. Oak was also used for the doors, staircases and floors, some of the wood was maturing for 50 years in his timber stores in St. James End. Outside tennis courts, large orchard and a delightful spinney. Today a lot of his buildings can be seen in Duston, quite a few around the New Duston Chapel also some of his excellent larger houses down Weedon Road. It is interesting that only the Duston estate was sold in 1919 but also most of the land between New and Old Duston was owned by Watkin Bros.

New Duston Watkins Bricks

Hopping Hill Farm before the site was used for brick making was the largest farm in the area, with its enormous barns and cattle yards. One has often wondered where its unusual name came from. Certainly not from the obvious explanation. Looking at some lists of county records some years ago I came across the name Hoppin, farmer, could this be the explanation. This could be the same as Bants Lane – Lodge Farm in the lower part of the lane when a Mr. Bantom farmed it. Then Watkin Bros. bought Hopping Hill for brick making, the works extended down to where is now Airflow's car site. Part of these works are still clad with the same red local pantiles. J.J. Watkin also built himself the Hopping Hill House, described then as the finest brick house in the county.

For the Steam Enthusiast

In 1890 a Fowler steam engine no. 6141 was used for powering the brick works and driving a Clayton Threshing Machine required for seasonal farm work and later a more powerful Charles Burrel engine built at Thetford no. 1594.

HOPPING HILL, DUSTON.
Near Northampton
(One-and-a-half miles from the Tram Terminus).

M E R R Y and C O.

Are instructed by the Executor of the late Mr. J. J. Watkin
TO SHORTLY SELL BY AUCTION:

Lot 1.–
THE MODERN SUBURBAN VILLA RESIDENCE,
containing excellent accommodation, built and occupied by the deceased owner, together with

Extensive Orchard
Ranges of Stabling,
Kitchen Garde,
Greenhouses, etc.

the whole containing about 12 ACRES.

Lot 2.–
A VERY VALUABLE PROPERTY,
Consisting of
FARMYARD and BUILDINGS,
FOUR COTTAGES, and long frontage to the main road.
AN EXCEPTIONAL BED OF CLAY,
BRICKYARD and PREMISES, Brick Kilns, Drying Sheds.
LIME PIT and LIME KILNS,
FOREMAN'S COTTAGE.
and FOUR CLOSES OF LAND,
in all about 40½ ACRES.

LOT 3.–
A SMALL ACCOMMODATION FARM,
with long building frontage to the road leading from Northampton to Harlestone, having a Cottage on same and a Sand Pit, the whole containing about 23 ACRES.

Lot 4.–
THREE ENCLOSURES OF LAND.
having about a quarter of a mile frontage to the road, leading from Old Duston to New Duston, forming fine buildings sites, the whole containing 32¼ ACRES.

Lot 5.–
A RESIDENTIAL BUILDING SITE,
situated on the main road from Northampton to Harleston, suitable for the erection of a
SUBURBAN VILLA.

Lot 6.–
A CLOSE OF ARABLE LAND,
having a long frontage to Bants Lane, leading from Old Duston to the main road from Northampton to New Duston, containing about 11 1/2 ACRES.

Full particulars, plans, and conditions of sale will shortly be ready, and may be obtained from the Auctioneers, Barclays Bank Chambers, St. Giles'-square, or from
Messrs. BECKE, GREEN, and STOPS
Solicitors,
Market-square, Northampton.

DUSTON PROPERTY SALE.

HOPPING HILL BOUGHT BY THE MAYOR.

The estate of the late Mr. J. J. Watkin at Hopping Hill, Duston, was offered for sale by auction at the Grand Hotel on Saturday by Messrs. Merry and Co. Five out of the eight lots were withdrawn. Messrs. Becke, Green and Stops were the solicitors.

Lot 1, the residence known as Hopping Hill, one-and-a-quarter miles from the Northampton tram terminus, a massive structure of brick with excellent rooms, orchard, stabling and glass houses, etc., the whole comprising an area of 11a. 3r. 2p. was sold to the Mayor (Councillor J. J. Martin, J.P.) for £5,350. Bidding started at £3,000.

Mr. Martin also bought the close of arable land known as Fox's Field on the road from Old Duston to the main Northampton–New Duston road, and containing 11a. 2r. 37p.

Lot 2, described as a very valuable property, consisting of farm, yard and buildings (carpenter's, paint and blacksmith's shops, cart hovel, large Dutch barn, etc.), a range of buildings, consisting of stable, boiler-house, granary, etc.; a foddering yard, four cottages, and, the most important feature of the lot, an exceptional bed of clay, from which one of the best known bricks can be produced, was first bid for at £5,000, and was sold to Mr. E. Travis at £9,750.

The brickyard premises on the lot comprised a 12-bay drying shed on brick piers and a five-bay range of very long drying sheds, an engine-room, two brick-kilns, and 70ft. shaft, a lime pit, and two lime-kilns. There was also a foreman's cottage and five closes of land.

Lot 3, a small accommodation farm known as Tucker's Lodge, was withdrawn at £1,700.

Three enclosures of land, one arable and two pasture, containing 32 acres 1 rood, were withdrawn at £2,300.

Three residential building sites on the main road of Northampton to Harleston, of one acre each, were withdrawn, £350 being bid for the first and no bids forthcoming for the others.

Taken from Northampton Mercury, 1919

Doddridge Castle Hill Chapel. A fine example of Duston Stone.

1965

Mr. Rushman's house and gardens, Port Road (now demolished).

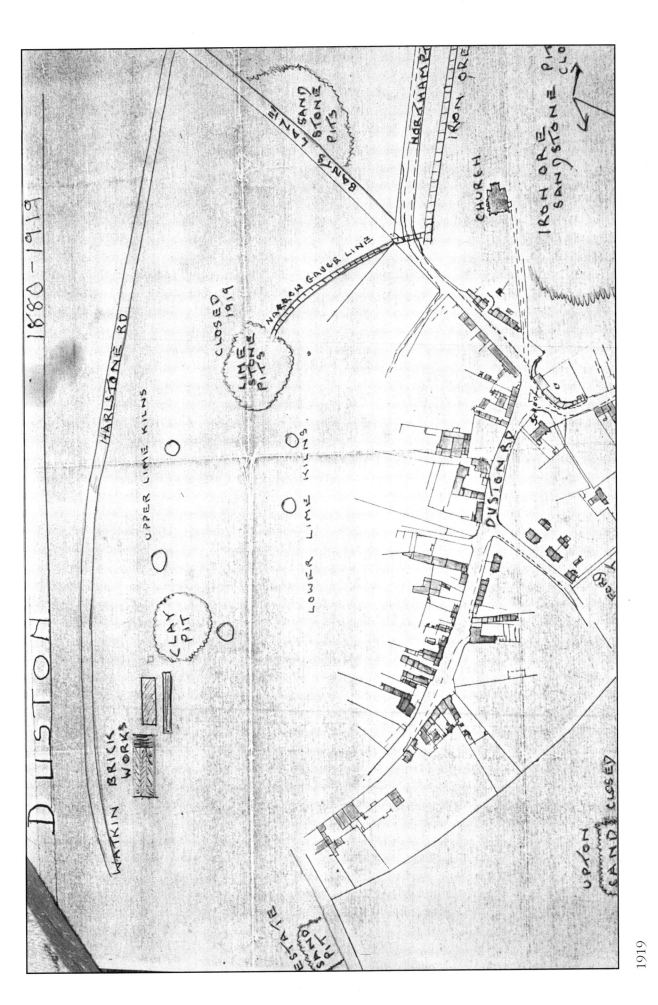

1919

Plan of Duston Stone Pits.

Part 4 – Old Duston St. James

There are no records that tell us much about old St. James End as distinct from the old parishes of Duston and Dallington. The Saxons are said to have erected a fort on the town side of the River Nene and there were one dwelling on the west bank during the existence of the Castle to help safeguard the crossing. Before the eastern parts of Dallington and Duston parishes formed the first St. James Parish there was a cluster of houses on the western bank of the Nene in Queen Elizabeth's reign then part of the old town. John Bunyan is reported to have preached there. From History of Doddridge Memorial – "There was a cluster of houses in the neighbourhood of the "Green Man" which in its heyday was a hostelry of some note. Between its huddle of houses and the ruined Castle walls which frowned down upon the Naseby branch of the Nene lay a strip of waste moor which was invariably flooded in winter. If the borough police ventured across the Narrow West Bridge in winter from "Black Lion" Hill they were faced with jeers and gaunts from its inhabitants". There was a Hermitage during the years of St. James Abbey at the river crossing bringing help and succour to the destitute and weary travellers.

In 1866 Rev. Lewis Clayton was sent by the Peterborough diocese to examine and prepare for the coming Anglian Church needs of the growing population of St. James. His beginning was a trial indeed having first to find his own accommodation had to look for a possible site for a School and Church, and set up the parochial organisations to go with them, his starting salary was £150 per year. The first year of his responsibilities was most unfortunate as smallpox raged in the town. In 1870 after great sacrifice and devotion he himself was stricken with the disease but he was able to survive and see the results of his endeavours, and see the first part of the St. James Schools built in 1870. In the main road the larger room of the east end dedicated for Sunday worship until the present Church was built.

Land for Victoria Park was acquired by the then District Council in commemoration of Queen Victoria's Jubilee, partly by a gift of Lord Spencer and partly by purchase altogether some 10 acres valued then at £1,800. By the mid 19th Century expansion of the boot and shoe industry from the town into St. James large areas for workers housing began to appear. In 1871 St. James was made an Urban District Council with Far Cotton and Dallington. In 1895 each of the three parishes had grown in population that each was declared a separate District Council. St. James in 1891 had a population of 4,159 with a total of 360 acres by 1899 a population of 6,500.

The District Council built the sewage works adjoining Victoria Park for the sum of £4,684.4.8d in 1879 (this was demolished only in recent years (after years of disuse).

The first meeting of St. James Urban District Council after the dissolved combined Council of 3 was held in St. James Cafe 8th April 1896 with Alfred Orton in the chair and Mr. Whitford, Mr E. Lewis, Mr. Gilbert and Mr. J. Parker.

The clerk was directed to appoint a Sanatory officer at a salary of £15 per annum. Inspector of nuisances at £17 per annum, a Surveyor at £30 per annum and a Rate Collector at £26 per annum. The following expenses for assessing the rate were interesting. 300 tons of Granite at 8s. 9d ton £131-5-0 Curb Stones at 8/- £40-0-0.

Wages for Warwick & Dunchurch Roads £80-0-0 Horse Carting £42, Footpaths £50.

Having to be brought up in Alma Street my education began and ended in St. James Church of England School built in 1873, this was continually enlarged to accommodate the increasing population of the new Northampton.

Old Dallington St. James

By 1895 the development of the outer western part of the town had been extended with shoe factories and associated tanning companys ect. together with dense housing that the first part of St. James was formed from Dallington and Duston Parishes. Spencer Land then began from the West Bridge and all land continuing with the railway on the one side and St. James Houses Road or Weedon Road on the other. Robert Spencer had a clause in the land sales that all houses built on this land with rear access service road ways (were to be provided) examples of this are in Symington Street, Newcombe Road, Argyle Street, Wimbledon Street, Althorpe Road ect. Park Road was originally the Dallington Northampton Estate, Town Road. From West Bridge across to the River Nene beyond St. James End Mill or Duston Lower Mill on to Duston Upper Mill was Duston Parish its northern boundary the Weedon Road all the development area to the "Red House" was included in the new parish of Northampton. In the early part of the 18th century just a hamlet called St. James End was considered a no go area where crime was prevalent was just over West Bridge. Duston Village School was opened by Lord Palmerstone, Lord of the Manor who succeeded the last Lord Melbourne (two of Queen Victoria's Prime Ministers) in 1856 prior to its opening children especially from St. James End walked all the way to Dallington village school built some 15 years earlier. Terrible flooding occurred in St. James before the last war a sea of water stretching from West Bridge to Marlborough Road after prolonged heavy rain, carts and the occasional boat was the mode of transport. The whole of the six fields from Abbey Street to Duston Mill was a sea and if this remained so in the depth of winter it was an added pleasure for we kids when frozen over. The industrial area of St. James has now seen great changes, most of the large boot and shoe factories have gone (Churchs Factory remains). One remembers the tanneries with their dreadful smells of the leather being treated, in awesome looking pits. On the open decker trams, noses had to be held as they passed the one near West Bridge, if there was a prevailing wind. It is recorded that some 5,000 people were employed directly or indirectly in St. James, in leather. The memories of my early days going into the ground floor of one of the largest factories (now gone) where the heavy belt driven machinery there was, every body was lip reading and the awful piece work. The smell of the leather still pregnated in them even in their best Sunday suit. Consolation was in drinking and backing horses. It is said that in a large factory you could find a bookies runner to take bets on every floor.

Barges worked their way from the canal at South Bridge to the narrow waterways round the old malt house at West Bridge and a large timber yard (prior to the Borough West Bridge Depot), moorings rings are still to be seen on the building.

As the industry and housing grew, so did the Non Conformist opposition to having to send their children to a church controlled school. Eventually a compromise was reached and a temporary Council School was built after the first war on the site, now part of the bus depot, this was a temporary solution to the problem. Built of corrugated iron and known as the tin school it was demolished when Gladstone Road School was built and pupils transferred there.

1908

Dallington Hall when Hon. Charles Robert Spencer lived there before he became 6th Earl Spencer to reside at Althorpe.

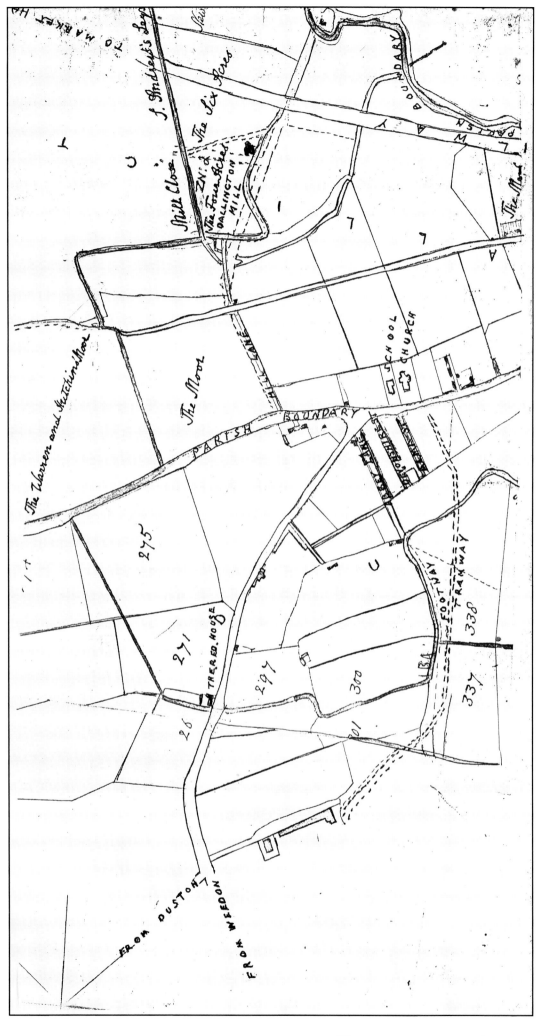

Old estate map of 1871 showing former Dallington parish land, the improvements of Dallington Mill Lane (Now Spencer Bridge Road) as far as Andrews Road, and the Old Duston Road Parish Boundary.

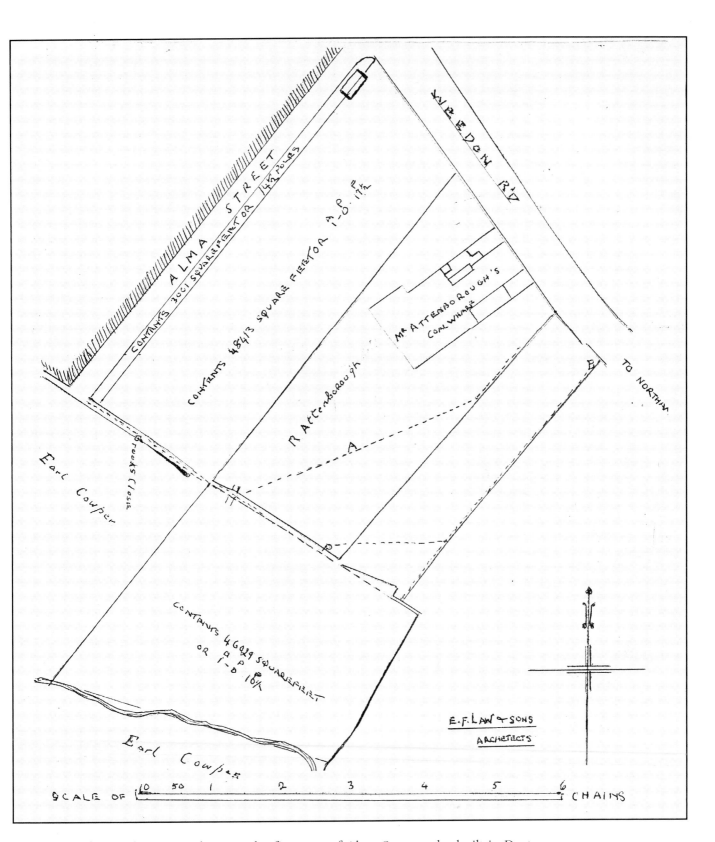

Plan drawn for Lord Cowper showing the first part of Alma Street to be built in Duston.

The Old Bants Lane Parish Boundary cast iron marker before Duston came into the Borough of Northampton.

These houses built on the old Spencer Land of Dallington in Old St. James all had access for supplies of coal etc.

1907

General Store
Lower Symington Street.

1920

Part of overhead hoist for
unloading grain in Westbridge
Granary many years ago.

1920

Old Granary West Bridge where grain barges used to moor and
unload.

1963

3 shops on St James Square including Mr. Green's who was always available administering help for our cuts and bruises to the children for over 50 years.

In the late 1960s these three properties were pulled down for road widening on St. James Sq. Police Station, Parrs (Car Spares) (old toll house), Mitchells (butchers), and Gunthorpe (Grocer).

Church & Co. Ltd.

Church & Co. Ltd. are internationally famous for their quality boots and shoes. From small beginnings this family business was begun in Duke St. by Mr. Alfred Church in partnership with his brothers Mr. Thomas Church and Mr. William Church. The original factory was extended several times then other premises in the town were used. In 1957 the move was made to the more commodious premises in St. James. This very large factory had been the home of Padmore & Barnes who originated from the North of England for many years.

The new factory was modernised and equipped with the modern machinery under the control of Mr. Leslie Church son of Alfred Church.

The closing dept had its own training dept and a nursery dept to facilitate the return to work of qualified closers who were married and had young children. Stages in the development of the business saw it converted to a private limited company in 1926 and a public company in 1951. After 1945 the company embarked on a policy of entering the retail trade with a view to maintaining adequate distribution of their shoes throughout the United Kingdom. So arrangements were made for leasing shoe departments in many large stores such as Austin Reed and other mens outfitters. In 1955 Church's acquired the firms of a Jones & Son Bootmakers Ltd. and this is now their own retail division.

Some 42 shops were operating from this combined acquisition in 1965.

A new company was added in the north of England for the retailing of high grade shoes Church-Allan Ltd in 1956 (Messrs James Allan & Son Ltd. of 123 Princes St. Edinburgh) who already had shops in Scotland, Church's also own the manufacturing and distribution rights of Mcafee of Dover St. W. London whose products sell world wide although Church's began exporting their footwear to America as early as 1921. They are firmly established as the leading exporters to the States of high quality boots and shoes. The first retail store was established in 1929 by Leslie Church, the former chairman. In 1959 retail outlets here opened in California. 1960 saw the first store opened in New York by 1986. Some so were in operation abroad and over 100 by Church & Co. (Footwear Ltd.) and their subsidiary companies.

An unforgettable day and a joint reward for the company's export expansion was the visit in July 1965 of H.M. the Queen and the Duke of Edinburgh to the St. James factory. There was an atmosphere as all St. James gathered outside the main road offices to see her majesty. All the area was with bunting shops and offices bedecked with flowers. In the boardroom the guests assembled. Representatives of the firms companies from worldwide. Mr. Leslie Church, Mr. Stewart Kennedy (chairman), Mr. Ian Church (vice-chairman) awaiting to accept their guests. Great interest was shown by the Duke in all the departments and to all employees in their various shoe crafts. Six year old Annabel, daughter of Mr. and Mrs. Ian Church presented Her Majesty with a bouquet and then smiling and waving they departed. A truly memorable day for Church & Co.

1973. Church & Co. celebrated their centennial year of trading and manufacturing footwear. 200 guests from all over the world including friends and colleagues of the company attended a luncheon at the Saxon Inn in Northampton. All employees later enjoyed a celebration evening with the company directors to mark this momentous occasion.

Today the factories are busy at full capacity. One of the few remaining boot and shoe firms left in Northampton a town that once upon a time the bulk of its citizens leather was their trade and occupation. The family tradition lives on. John Church is chairman of the parent Co. (Church & Co. plc.) and Ian Church is on the board of directors, both grandsons of the founders.

C and E Lewis Progressive Works

Edward Lewis was born in Northampton in 1861. At the age of ten he began to work for a farmer. He came of Welsh stock, his parents lived in Old Devonshire Street, both are buried in Duston Churchyard, from very small beginnings and with very little money Edward and his brother Charles began a small boot and shoe business in Tanner Lane 1872. While Edward travelled for orders his brother attended to the manufacturing side which was the enterprising ability and also attention to all departments of this enterprising firm that after acquiring a number of small factories. They eventually built the large "Progressive works" in St. James and it opened in 1894 when his younger brother T.D. Lewis became a partner. As a large employers of labour they endeavoured to share the success with their personnel in the form of bonus schemes. Edward held strong views on religious, political and social subjects.

St. James had a great benefactor in Edward Lewis in provided his gift of Dallington Park in conjunction with his brothers Charles and T.D. Lewis. All were generous in their support of Doddridge Memorial Church.

Edward held high office in associated organisations in Northampton. T.D. Lewis and Edward both were J.P.s, both elected town councillors and dully held the high office of Mayor, Edward 1903. T.D. 1923. Edward died 1927 in Oaklands his home opposite the lower entrance to Dallington Park, from Harlestone Road and St. James Road to Doddridge Memorial the long funeral cortege of vehicles decked with flowers was seen by crowds of people paying their last respects to a true citizen of St. James. Over a hundred wreaths were laid out on his lawns for the mourners to view.

I have written a lot more concerning Edward Lewis to be found in other pages of the History of St. James.

Colliers Factory

Simon Collier was born in Great Russell Street 1839 his father Alderman William Collier was an established boot and shoe manufacturer. He was educated at Northampton Grammar school later trained in his fathers business. He later kept "The Woolpack" (now gone) licenced premises in Bridge Street went into business in Wolverhampton for a time but finally returned to boot and shoemaking in a small way in Freehold Street in 1880. So successful did he soon become that by 1898 the first large factory to be built in St. James employing 200 people and by the first war trebling that number. Simon Collier Ltd. was now well established and in 1898 the firm was converted to a Limited Liability Company the directors being Mr. Simon Collier, Mr. Charles Collier, Mr. J. V. Collier, Mr. J. L. Collier and Mr. W. V. Collier all shares retained in the family. During the 1914-1918 war this large factory was reorganised to the production of Army Boots some 3000 pairs produced daily. Simon was highly esteemed as an employer and business man. He, like the other prominent boot and shoe manufacturers of St. James soon began to take part in the affairs of the town. He was chairman of St. James Ward Conservative Association in 1902, and in the same year was returned a successful candidate for St. James Ward. He was one of the directors of Northampton Tramways Company he helped in the negotiation leading to the purchase of the company by the corporation in 1901. He later became chairman of the tramway committee in 1901.

His son Charles Collier (he died in 1906) was for many years resident representative in South Africa where a large part of the factory production continued to be exported between the wars. Simon Collier died in 1928 aged 91 in "Thornbank", his Dallington Home.

His funeral took place at St. Luke's Duston where for many years he had been a constant worshipper, he is buried with his family outside the East Wall of the Chancel.

The Whitton Last Works

Well over a hundred years ago in 1878 Robert Whitton first began his "last" and boot "tree" business in Inkerman Terrace, Northampton. He lived in Castillian Street and the factories have always born the name Castillian Last Works. His son Charles Robert continued the expanding business from St. Giles Street premises by the turn of the century. By 1905 still further larger site was sought so he began building in St. James Road and for many years the combination of the timber works, kilns etc. The wood turning and carving was in the town factory which continued until 1932 when a more up to date working factory was completed, displaying its product of "Last" on the front of the premises. Charles built himself a fine house on the Weedon Road opposite the "Tap" (this was a beer house at the entrance to Melbourne Road and served beer on one side, and in the old Salon Dance Hall when in use.)

Always gentlemanly dressed complete with bowler hat he would be driven in his car each morning to his office and works. Mr. Whitton tells me years ago English hard wood beech was used and it arrived at the factory in long tree lengths and was cut up into various sizes and thicknesses suitable for lasts. Each end was dipped in cow manure he said, to stop cracking, then steamed, kilned and dried. Then, when some 100 men were employed all shaping was done by knife, and rasp, and spokes. Often one pair of wooden lasts were sent to an ironworks to produce a certain size iron last, from which a quantity could be produced for factory use. Wooden lasts could be seen on the shelves of the high class shoe stops where a customer ordered a pair of shoes or boots to be made to his or her size.

Part of the old works still stand where women used to make fibre filler lasts for window shop display. These were made by placing fibre board round a slightly smaller wooden last then baked and for some shoe companies in brown or black celluloid. So large quantities of these light weight shoe lasts could be produced for displaying high quality boots and shoes. Before 1939 cheaper shoes were 12/6 the best £1.1.0d. Wood for the lasts today is imported, American Maple, all ready for machining and treated, and dried to a moisture content of 7% in various block sizes. Let us wish Mr. Robert Whitton every success in containing this highly skilled wood craft passed on through three generations from his Grandfather.

1926

Messrs Lewis's Finishing Room

1909

The gas making plant of Marlows Factory. Then they had to provide their own gas for power and dig deep wells for water.

1939

Shoe "last" as made from a block of Canadian Maple at St James Road last factory.

1920

A wooden "last" made for a military cap at St James Road last factory.

FIRST and ALWAYS

THE 'LASTMAN'

Over 75 years service to the trade.

R. WHITTON
CASTILLIAN LAST WORKS
NORTHAMPTON
TELEPHONE: 97

1953
A finished "last" taken from a brochure of 1953 when the company had a factory in Castillian Street, Northampton

1921

Lewis's heavy belted machinery ground floor.

Horse Trams

The trams in St. James began some years before the electric trams in 1904 when horses provided the power to bring the crowds to Franklins Gardens to enjoy the recreation and sporting activities there returning to town the sweating horses, pulling a full tram up Black Lion Hill. All vehicles were painted one colour for one route in town and the destinations painted on the sides the interiors lit at night with oil lamps in the very foggy weather bells were attached to the horses, some nasty accidents happened to the animals in the winter when animals lost their grip on the ice and before the driver could apply the brakes of the tram hit them.

Over a hundred horses were looked after in the Ridings of Abington St. Each had to work some 4 hours at a stretch. These few notes are taken from Drivers and Conductors remembrances of horse trams from old Northampton Independent's all agreed that it was a blessing when Electric Trams replaced the Horse Trams, although they recalled all animals were well fed, groomed and stabled individually.

Trams

The tram depots down St. James began its operating life in 1904. The Northampton Borough Council purchased the old house tramways from a private company in 1901 for £37,000. This old building is still part of the busy Corporation Bus Depot and is significant by its curvature headed vehicle entrance. This original tram building was built by Watkins Bros. who had their extensive brickworks at New Duston. The buildings now all stand on the Old Stensons Iron Works site of some 11 and a half acres that closed down in 1880. Stenson Street still opposite (once Foundry Street) and Foundryman Arms (once Foundry Arms) remain.

As a boy I remember the flashes of light as dozens of trams in the early morning came out of the sheds and were reconnected to the overhead power by the conductor man connecting the cable arm on to the overhead wire for the required journey. We thought it was great fun to snowball the poor passengers on the top of the open trams, the tram driver standing with no protection except a heavy overcoat covered in driving snow. It was some years before better covered trams were in service. I have mentioned before, the long line of trams at the terminal at Franklins Gardens, waiting for the end of an important match when the last of the trams in the line had to be the first to be away, backed to town so crammed, that the conductor could only take one penny fare. As they clambered off the last tram from town at night "Depot Only" the conductor called eagerly taking the fare, before anyone went upstairs as he entered his total fares on his pad, and began to put his money in respective money bags to complete his day. *From the London Municipal Journal 1904 Northampton Tramways*. "The total cost of the reconstruction scheme is estimated at £85,000. The Borough Council need an estimated revenue of £17,000 a year to show a profit which is £6,000 more than the horsed lines. The streets are far from ideal for tramways purposes. They are wide in the less congested parts, where they might be narrower, and they are narrow in the centre, where traffic requirements demand they shall be wide. The Council is gradually improving the condition of affairs by widening, but these operations are single lines in many streets where ought really to be double ones. If the town be wise, it will in a very short time endeavour to extent its tramway system by constructing a light railway at least to Wellingborough, and to Kettering if possible. The linking up of these towns with the county town would add enormously to the prosperity of all. The present railway service is not convenient and farmers' goods between Northampton and Wellingborough are spoiling for efficient means of transport to the county town. Northampton's position as an agricultural centre is visibly declining, but it would be made proof against the competition of all comers were the tramway system now inaugurated judiciously extended. These extensions would produce another effect, that of assisting the solution of the housing problem. General experience has been that the earning capacity of electric traction is much greater than that of horse tractions. The borough engineer (Mr. Fidler) has carried through the scheme without the assistance of an outside consulting engineer and the work is of an excellent character throughout. The Council has now 20 cars with a carrying capacity of 48 each, as compared with 14 of 28 each under the old enterprise. Penny fares are universal, and with the much quicker service there should be no question as to financial success.

The route length of the tramway is about 5 and a half miles equal to about nine miles of single track. The actual commencement of the work was made in January, and over several portion of the routes the traffic on the existing tramways was continued. The whole of the sections are completed with the exception of the Kingsthorpe Section, which it is expected will be finished before the end of the month. For various reasons it was decided to maintain the existing gauge of 3ft. 6in. Where found to be sound, the existing concrete foundations were used, and for all new foundations cement concrete of the proportion of five parts of broken stone, one part of sand, one part of Portland cement, was used. The rails are of the girder type, 6 and a half in. deep, weighing 90 lbs. per yard for the straight rails and 96lb. per yard for the curved rails, and the fish-plates weight 50 lbs. per pair, having six bolt holes. The rails and fish-plates were supplied by the North Eastern Steel Company, Middlesborough. Mild steel tie-bars were used, and at each rail joint and midway in the length of the rail anchor sole-plates were used to secure the rails to the concrete foundations.

The points and crossings were manufactured by Messrs. Askham Brothers and Wilson of Sheffield. They are of cast crucible steel, with forged steel tongues. The movable points are of the automatic spring type, and are interchangeable. The points are 12 ft. in length, and the crossings are of iron bound type, the arms being of similar rail section securely embedded in the castings. The rails are drained where necessary by means of drain boxes discharging into adjacent branch drains. The rails are bonded at every joint with protected copper bonds, the cross bonds being of solid copper of the Neptune type. The permanent way is paved partly with Norwegian granite setts, and for the remainder with the old setts taken up from the existing tramways and redressed, the joints being grouted with Portland cement and sand.

From economical motives it was decided to erect the power station upon ground adjacent to the refused destructor in Castle Street, in order to utilise the steam raised by the destruction of the town refuse by the dust destructor, the central position of which enabled a more economical distribution of current throughout the system. The engine room is 63ft. long, 40 ft. wide, and 22 ft. 3 in. high to the tie-rod of the rood trusses. The boiler house is 46 ft. 3 in. long, 38 ft. wide, and 14 ft. 6 in. high. These measurements are over all, and include pump room, mechanical draught room and accommodation for coal. The store room is 38 ft. long and 18 ft. 7 and a half in. wide. A similar space is devoted to the mechanics' shop and engineer in charge. Over these rooms is the battery room, 38 ft. long and 38 ft. wide and 9 ft. high to the tie-beam, with steel and concrete composite floor. The engineer's office, general office, and testing room are each 12 ft. by 12 ft. 5 in. by 14ft high. There are two sets of bathrooms and lavatory accommodation, 18 ft. 6 in. by 10 ft. 10 in. over all. The exterior of the building is of selected brickwork with terra-cotta and stone facing blue Staffordshire brick dado and plinth. The engine-room floor is laid with red tiles diagonally. The engineer's office floor is laid with wood blocks. The roof of the building is covered with Mellowes patent glazing and the portions near the eaves are slated over diagonally with boarding.

The existing plant at the refuse destructor consists of two steel Lancashire boilers, 30 ft. long and 8 ft. in diameter, suitable for working to 160 lb. pressure, with a Green's economiser for feed water heating. The steam raising plant in the new power station consists of two boilers of the Economic type, each capable of evaporating 8,000 lb. of water per hour and made by Messrs. Davey, Paxman and Co. of Colchester. The boilers are fitted with mechanical stokers of the Bennis type, and superheaters are placed in the boiler flues capable of superheater the steam to 500deg. Fahr.

The generating plant consists of two 200k.w. sets composed of Williams compound 3-crank engine, of 350 revolutions per minute, capable of giving 360 I.H.P., and an International Electrical Company's dynamo; also one compound set, capable of giving an output of 120 k.w., consisting of a Williams two-crank compound engine of 350 revolutions per minute, capable of giving 240 I.H.P., and a dynamo of the International Electrical Engineering Company's make. The battery was made by Messrs. Ashmore, Benson and Peace of Stockton-on-Tees. It consists of 250 cells, and is capable of giving out 170 amperes for three hours. There is also provided a reversible booster and milking set, both made by the International Electrical Engineering Company.

The overhead equipment is to a great extent on the span-wire principle, with brackets arm construction in the narrow streets. The poles are of lapwelded steel, in three sections, telescoped into each other, and have an ornamental wrought-iron base, bearing the borough coat-of-arms. The span-wirepoles have curved wrought-iron scroll work, and the bracket arms have ornamental iron scroll work supports.

There are 20 cars of the following dimensions: – Length of car body 16ft.; over all length, 26 ft.; total over all width, 6 ft. 4 in. They are all of the single truck double deck type. The framing is of oak, the floor of pine, the dashers of steel plates, the stairway stringers of sheet steel firmly bolted to the car body and platform. The handrails are of brass tubing. The cars are provided with an effective system of lighting, with head lights, signal lights, and lights for the destination indicators. The cars are handsomely finished in an artistic fashion, the waist being rich crimson with gold panelled borders, the remainder of the body being cream. At each end of the car an automatic safety guard of the Hudson and Bowring type is fitted."

The contractors for the various sections were as follows:-

Boilers condensing plant, the British Westinghouse Electric and Manufacturing Company, Manchester: steam generators, dynamos, battery, the International Electrical Engineering Company, London; the overhead trolley equipment, the Brush Electrical Engineering Company, Limited, London: underground feeder cables and pilot wires, Messrs. Siemens Brothers and Co, Limited, London; cars Messrs. Dick Kerr and Co., Limited, Preston; permanent way, Messes. J.G. White and Co. Limited, London; power-station, W. Beardsmore, Northampton.

Gentlemen responsible for the Electric Tramway System were councillor Edward Lewis (Mayor). Aldeman, Wooding (Chairman of the tramway committee). Mr. Hankinson (Town Clerk). Mr. Goth (Tramways General Manager). Mr. A. Fidler (Borough Engineer). Mr. J. McMahon (Electrical Engineers.)

1904

Tram sheds St. James Road drivers, conductors and maintenance staff.

1904

Newly built tram sheds, St. James Road (now part of the town bus depot)

1904

The opening ceremony of the electric tram depot at St. James.

1904

A tribute. The passing of the horse trams.

Abbey Works

In 1770 Mr. William Smith began an engineering business at 69, Princes Street, London, the present site of the Prince of Wales Theatre.

He invented an oil door closer with spring named "Janus" still being made in the 1970's.

His succeeding family together with A. Smith and Mr. Stevens made by 1880 at Queens Road, Battersea hand powered and hydraulic lifts, also rope stranding machines. 1909 Charles Major joined the firm so it became Smith, Major and Stevens (Smith Majors to the St. James employees) and so they came to Northampton. The site chosen was Abbey Park planned as an extension of Franklins Gardens by Mr. Franklin which never came to fruition. Mr. Franklin sold all his assets in Northampton in 1889. By 1909 this fine engineering works was completed to employ some 280 people (during the building operations various stone coffins were found) then the contribution to the town a large expanding engineering firm coming to employ local labouring predominant boot and shoe area was a matter for much congratulation. Something very pleasing too was its sport facilities. Cricket Club, Bowls and Athletic Club all planned so that the frontal part of the premises gave a garden effect.

1917 saw an amalgamation of the Easton Electric Company together with The General Electric Company to form the Express Lift Company.

In 1930 Smith Major Stevens was merged with Express Lift Co. Ltd with the backing of G.E.C., after 1935 G.E.C. acquired the whole of the share capital.

In 1932 it was decided to erect a test tower 60 ft high, this corrugated iron tower rising above the works we recall, it stood for over 40 years.

By 1930 Express Lift Company had been formed with backing of G.E.C., and Northampton became the main administrative centre of the new company the beginning of the collaborated large world wide company it is today. The largest British controlled lift manufactured company.

Mr. V. Amberg who was the head of G.E.C. Telephone Company of Coventry was asked by Lord Hirst to take over the running of the Express Lift of Northampton. The Year after in 1954 he was appointed Associate Director of General Electric Company. Mr. V Amberg who lived at the "Chantry" in Duston was noted for various activities, he was commander of the Duston Home Guard here 1939-1945. Mr. P.C. Major another director whose father helped the company form, built himself a fine large stone house in 1930, still named "Ashtrees" and in the parks ran a sizeable Mushroom farm. The main drive is now Saxon Rise with the Lodge House still standing at the old entrance.

The test tower erected in 1932 was built in the middle of the block of buildings and was used to develop high speed gearless lifts of the day.

1980 saw the remarkable giant lift testing tower being built. This enormous structure now a well known landmark was a remarkable undertaking 400 ft. high 14.6 meters in diameter at the base, and 8.5 meters at the top. The total height was achieved and built in 4 weeks. The total weight 4,000 tonnes. There are three tall shafts inside the tower, one to carry the engineers, (safety lift) and with a travel of 113 meters serving 19 levels at 1.6 meters per second. A high shaft of 120 meters for testing to 10 meters per second. The third shaft gives 4 independent lift facilities by dividing the shaft into sections for training purposes. A fourth shaft of 32 meters is there for type testing. It is a delightful experience to join a group on a visit to this wonderful structure and to view Northampton. The tower today is a landmark for the town and a monument to the original Smith Major and Stevens who came here nearly a hundred years ago.

The Tower was opened on the 12th November 1982 by Her Majesty Queen Elizabeth II, at the time when Mr. M. Dove was Managing Director, and Mr R. J. Bedford, the driving force behind the building of the tower, was the Engineering Director.

1900

Abbey Works Office Block.

Some of the old St. James Abbey worked stone can be seen built into 17th Century cottages in the old village thought to have come from the Escpiness Abbey Works site.

Stensons Ironworks

Erected for Joseph Stenson in 1853 some 100 men were employed there (afterwards the Corporation Transport Depot occupied the site) producing 200,000 tons of pig iron annually. The works were supplied by a full gauge iron ore line connected to the Peterborough to Blisworth L.N.W. railway at Duston West Junction. From there the line was elevated on heavy timbers across the upper Nene flood plain to a high bank (locally known as the High lines) to a central depot off the Weedon Road, another line came off this junction to pits as far as Duston Church. Then one mile of track to St. James it made its way round the rear of Franklins Gardens across the fields to what is now Lincoln Road (the rail bank from Abbey Street is still there) terminating left into what is now Spencer Street so supplying a large brick and coal wharf next to the foundry this length of line was taken up from the Weedon Road Central Depot soon after the Castle Station was built. The main iron ore line operated much longer till 1909.

The old engine sheds have now been demolished and the site is now part of Ross Way Industrial buildings.

Some years ago I photographed the old buildings typical of early 19th century industrial factory with its iron window frames and small glass panes. The inspection pit was still there and across the eaves supporting the roof was a 20ft long large thick wooden plank used in the ore pits for wheeling away the overburden (top soil and sub soil) over the pits away on to already extracted site, along the centre of the timber is a deep grove the result of endless hours of men wheeling heavy barrows with iron wheels often 20 ft or more above ground so delicate was this operation that men and barrow could tip over and serious injury occur, but back to Stensons. High on the wall at the east end of Stenson Street painted and still readable is the old Foundry Street name the old pub built as "Foundry Arms" and the "Forge Hammer" in Alma Street together help quench the thirst of the foundry workers. Here are copies of documents relating to the subsequent changes of ownership and disposal of relating materials.

Here is a list tracing the various owners of the Ironworks to the closure.

1878   Sale of Ironworks by Original Owners.
1883   The Whitworth family of Dallington were in possession.
1889   Converting to John Beck and Allchin Linnell and Co. Ltd. taking over the site.
1892   Letters mentioning the sale by Messrs Allchin & Co. of the works to G. Spokes Engineer, also the original ownership of the tracks verified by Mr. Garratt Estate agent to Lord Cowper, Lord of the Manor, both letters concerning John Beck.
1900   Final close of St. James branch line and disposal of tracks.

"This indenture made the fourteenth day July between Richard Attenborough of Reading in the family of Berks Merchant, of the one part and Anne Whitworth of Dallington Hall, Northamptonshire Widow of the other part where as by virtue of an Indenture dated the twenty seventh day of September One thousand eight hundred and eighty three and made between the Right Honorable Earl Cowper of the first part Thomas Battams Turnell of the second part and the said Richard Attenborough of the third part or by virtue of other acts deeds the said Richard Attenborough is entitled to certain rights, privileges in connection with certain Railways and Tramways used in connection with certain Ironworks and a wharf situated in St. James End in the Parish of Duston in the County of Northampton. And whereas the said Anne Whitworth has become the purchaser from the said Richard Attenborough of the said works and wharf and it was part of the terms of purchase by her from the said Richard Attenborough that he should assign such rights and privileges as aforesaid to the said Anne Whitworth and whereas it is intended to pay full in respect of the entire purchase money on the deed of conveyance bearing the date herewith thereby such works and wharf have been conveyed to the said Anne Whitworth. 'Now this indenture witneseth that in consideration of the promises the said Richard Attenborough doth hereby as beneficial convey and assign to the said Anne Whitworth 'All and singular the rights proves consents and privileges to which the said Richard Attenborough is entitled in respect of the aforesaid Railways and Tramways."

Memorandum of Agreement made this day October One thousand eight hundred and eighty nine between John Becke of Northampton Esquire of the one part and A Linnell and Company Limited of the other part supplemental to an agreement leaving date the twelfth day of October one thousand eight hundred and eighty nine and made between the same parties and herein after referred to the Original agreement.

The Purchases shall take to all the moveable of Iron whether manufactured or in course of manufacture and all the loose tools implements coal scrap steel and all other and things used in the made or business of the manufacture of Iron as now carried on at the works and which were not included in the original contract and also the stock of iron and the furniture now in the London Warehouse at the price of Five thousand nine hundred and forty seven pounds sixteen shillings and nine pence to be said as follows. Two thousand two hundred and sixty eight by a bill drawn by the vendor and accepted by the purchases and payable three months after date and the balance of three thousand six hundred and seventy nine pounds sixteen shillings and nine pence in Cash.

The Purchases having paid the deposit of Eight hundred Pounds under the original agreement all to be declined to have entered into possession of the twenty first day October last and they are to be at liberty to cancel on the works or not and to put up additional buildings, plants and machinery but not to pull down to remove any buildings and fixed plant now valued is put down until the whole of the purchase money payable under the original agreement has been paid or secured accordance with the loans of that Agreement.

The Purchasers are to carry out the contract entered into between the vendor and Messrs Butlin and Co. for the supply of Pig Iron to the vendor and the contract between the vendor and Messrs Howard of Bedford for the supply of finished iron Vendor so the said Messrs Howard and to indemnify the vendor from all claims under or in of such contract.

Stensons Iron Works
Northampton
May 7 1892

John Becke Esq J.s.
Billing Road
Northampton

Dear Sir,

I herewith enclose copy of a letter received from Mr. Garratt repeating the railway siding. I also enclose copy of the inventory relating to same of any purchase from Messrs Allchin & Co. Can you favor me with any particulars can claim the rail?

Earl Cowper

Yours faithfully

George Spokes

The whole of the railways from boundary gate throughout the works as laid on transverse sleepers in cast iron chairs comprising 433 lineal yards of permanent way with two crossings and one point and lever.

The whole of the railway from boundary gate to Duston brickyard comprising 845 yards of permanent way as laid on transverse sleepers and cast iron chairs.

The permanent way and siding to Saint James Coal Companys yard comprising 151 lineal yards of way with one crossing and two points and levers.

So with the loss of the rail link Stensons Ironworks came to an end. Part of the site was rebuilt for the tram depot and a temporary school (the tin school was built a large corrugated iron structure) many St. James people remember being taught there.

IRON WORKS SALE 1878

To Iron Manufacturers.—

To be Sold by Private Treaty, an Old-established Ironworks, for rolling best iron, consisting of Forge & Rolling Mills, with Plant & Machinery.

The Forge consists of eight Puddling Furnaces, two Ball Furnaces, a five-ton Helve Hammer, a five-ton double-action Steam Hammer (nearly new) & a powerful 20in Train, rolling 3in 4in 5in & 6in forge bars.

The Mills consist of one 14in & one 9in Train for merchant bars & one 8in Guide Train, with two Mill Furnaces.

The Machinery is driven by a fifty h-p Condensing Beam Engine of recent construction.

The Premises occupy rather more than 12½ Acres of Land, with a frontage of about 216 yards to the main road adjoining a large & flourishing town, & there is a communication by tramway with the L&NW-Railway.

Land Tax redeemed & tithe free.

A Sheet, Plate or Hoop Mill could be added at a very moderate outlay & the premises could be easily adapted for any work, requiring a large space.

The whole is now at work, & has for many years done a good trade in best brands & will be sold as a going concern.

Liberal arrangements as to payment.

The whole value of the land not including Plant & Machinery could remain on mortgage.

1878. Stensons Iron Foundry particulars of sale.

1967

Demolition of part of Stenson Street, once Foundry Street.

Site of Duston Canal Wharf where there was a rail link to the iron ore line to St. James.

Railways.

The whole of the railways from boundary gate throughout the works as laid on transverse sleepers in cast iron chairs comprising 433 lineal yards of permanent way with two crossings and one point and lever.

The whole of the railway from boundary gate to Duston brickyard comprising 845 yards of permanent way as laid on transverse sleepers and cast iron chairs.

The permanent way and siding to Saint James coal box yard comprising 151 lineal yards of way with one crossing and two points and levers.

1898

Closure of rail line to St. James. A letter outlining the quantity of railway track owned by Lord Cooper.

1875

Price list of iron and steel products of Stensons iron foundry St. James.

1892

Copy of letter to new owners of Stensons iron works regarding the estates branch line from central depot to St. James that used to supply the works.

Travis and Arnold

Travis and Arnold began the company's operation on a small site on the corner of Mill Road, St. James on the old Duston Main Road in 1907.

Mr. Travis having founded a small timber importing business in London in 1899. He later moved to Aylesbury where he met his future partner Mr. Arnold. After other branches had been added to the company the head office was established and the original partnership continued until 1937 when Mr. Ernest Travis died. He was succeeded by his son Mr. E. R. Travis who in 1949 became Chairman and Managing Director when the partnership became a private Limited Company. By 1944 the public were invited to purchase shares in the Company and from then on a series of acquisitions began. Today it is a giant with the founders grandson, Mr. Travis at the head of a partnership now Travis Perkins.

In the early days going for timber at Travis one remembers the wooden office buildings, the seasoned timber, the belted noisy saws all in one small area

Gandy's Bakeries

One of the largest bakery businesses in Northampton before the last war was Gandy in Park Road. Recently I had the pleasure of talking to the founders son who detailed his fathers successful career.

Born in 1874 he commenced his first tiny bakery in Artizan Road in 1904. He then moved to much larger premises in 1907, in Hunter Street. So renowned for his quality of cakes he proceeded to acquire land to the South End of Victoria Park and built much larger, productive premises and so began, in 1910, Victoria Bakery and continued for over 50 years.

I remember the huge ovens in the East End of the bakery, the prepared loaves were loaded on trolleys in the work area and being on iron wheels were pushed into the ovens. One remembers the large number of vans lined up in the yard for distribution all over Northampton. In 1924 he built on to the front premises a large and well equipped cake shop well patronised by St. James residents. They had four stalls in the centre of the market where trays of sugar coated sweets were sold, very well presented, with their nice white sheets back and front of the stalls and staff in their white aprons. The sweets were made in Roseholme Road opposite the County Ground under the management of Benjamin Benham he was a well known figure on the market for 50 years. The end of the market sweet stalls came around in 1906 when an order was made for every stallholder to comply with a health order, whereby all were compelled to purchase a metal container some 2 ½ ft x 18" with heating apparatus and a bowl in which to wash hands. Within a few months the idea was found impracticable and this order ended his sweet stall. In 1928 he thought he would diversify his interests and purchased land at Overstone, firstly building the Solarium swimming pool, then he built the large Hotel but failed to get a licence, so it was used for a social club for a number of years before obtaining a full licence.

A good deal of Horton House demolished stone, he had conveyed to the site, and was used in its construction.

St. James Abbey

The large complex of buildings that stood from the 12th century to the early part of the 16th century to the early part of the 16th century was walled in from the Duston Road of junction to the Weedon Road to Melbourne Lane. On the south side of Weedon "Bridges" writes, the Abbey seems to have stood on the descent from Duston to the south and south east, westwards is a wall of other stone near which are the foundations of the buildings". As further down on the lower land a brook made its way from Duston and supplied water for Abbotts Mill, also the great barn stood nearby.

Here the Town Clerk writing in the 17th century says, "The Abbey has a stately barn slatted on the west side supported by 12 buttrises. On the south side there are two large porches to enter the barn. "Rev. Sergeantson" writing in 1906 says "not a vestige of this remains, but a small section of the wall to to be seen on the Weedon Road near the spot where Upton and Duston Road divide".

I remember when the existing stone wall went up from the Express Lift tennis courts to opposite the Duston turn within this wall of the housing area of Abbotts Way and Peverals Way large blocks of stone and tiled floors were found as the foundations and gardens were begun. In the beginning the Abbey was dedicated to St. James by William Peveral for the order of Black Canons. He endowed it with 40 acres and a Mill in the same Parish. The Abbey was the order of St. Augustine. The charter was confirmed the founder died in 1113. A hundred years later the Rectories of Bozeat, Cranford, Heyford, Horton, Roade, Rothersthorpe, Watherley and Watford were appropriated to the Abbey also by then some 60 villages in the country had Abbey property. By 1154 all the estates of Peveral were confiscated for the treason of the founders grandson and the Manor of Duston was granted to Wakelin-de-Duston meanwhile Ralph who had become the first Abbott in 1158 left their first temporary church buildings probably of wood and occupied their new monastery buildings of stone. In 1223 a disastrous fire ruined a lot of the Abbey, Henry III helped the Canons by giving 30 rafters for rebuilding as the work was still not complete. Another gift was by the King of the two oaks were given for the building of the Church Tower. In 1229 the Abbott and Convent obtained from the King a grant to hold an annual fair in the Abbey. The morrow of St. James day (25th July) this fair survived the dissolution and was moved to Northampton Market Square in 1690 (some photography is available as it was held there up to the latter part of the 19th century). Walter Abbott of St. James died in 1237 Adam Gylby one of the Canons was to be the next Abbott although a signed approval was obtained from the King the Bishop of Lincoln would not authorise it, and after the Canons were again to hold an election their prior Osbert was given royal assent and a consent by the Bishop. 1292 all Jews were to be banished from England and their properties seized by the crown and in April of that year granted to the Abbey the site and various houses in Northampton including the Scola Synagogue and houses that were owned by Sarra of London a Jewess the former had a settlement, was close to the walls of the Abbey. 1299 the Abbott of St. James died (Ralph de Higham) two of the Canons were sent to the king as was the custom to notify the death of their Abbott and to get royal permission to elect another the two delegated duly returned with the royal letters. They returned to the King later with their approved choice with the consent of the Bishop of Lincoln Nicholas de Felore was made the new Abbott, he ruled for 34 years and he ernestly go to work rebuilding the Abbey Church that had begun by this predecessor. The King gave eight oaks in Salley Forest which had to be of the finest timber, the order to be carried out by this Justice of the Forest Rodger Lerangre. In 1301 a licence was granted permitting the dedication of two alters in the new Abbey Church. Two years later a similar licence was granted for the dedication to St. Margaret and St. Katherine is recorded. Wills and their contects make interesting reading. Walter Passelew in 1340 left, 6 shillings and 8 pence to the house. John Passelew of Northampton in 1349 a anum cistum to St. James and a seal to Canon Passelew of the Monastery. Many notable and worthy citizens of the town and county wished to be interned in the Abbey Church more than one Abbot is said to be buried in Duston Church which was in the care of St. James Abbey for several hundred years. In 1490 Richard Wordville, Earl Rives bequeathed his body to be buried in the Abbey Church. In 1488 John Catesby of Arthingworth also made the same request. 1501 Richard Berde doctor of law in the Monastery of St. James with his body to be buried in the conventual church he bequeathed his best gown and hood value £10 to recompense for the expenses incurred, 20s to the Abbot and 10s to each of the canons. He left 30/- to the poor of St. James End, Dallington and Duston viz 20/- in bread and 10/- in money, he also desired his executures to his large goblet and bowl his grat salt and for silverspoons and the money to go to the poor.

Nicholas-de-Flore died in 1334 after 36 years as Abbott. Nicholas was buried as history tells us in the Abbey Church but his tomb cover in Duston Church is one of the few artifacts remaining of the Abbey, it was removed from a position above ground level some 17 years ago where it had laid for long recorded years to a covered area in the clergy vestry its weight is 5 to 6 cwt, the full inscription on it, is as follows:

> Hie jaun in petra sculpta marmore tetra R. Flos de Flore gregis istius actus honore Pastor sublatus fuit hic et morigeratus Sit Christi natus anima (maque Deus miser) atus

Translation:

"Here lies in a stone coffin fashioned out of marble. Nicholas de Flore shepard of yonder flock now force from his office: exalted was he and withal considerate. May he prove a son of Christ and God have mercy on his soul."

He desired that John Mason the hermit have his printed mass book in his chapel to every poor child seeking alms in St. James Abbey 2d and every poor man of the same 4d. To fourteen of the servants of the Abbey he left 8d (all named) any other servant 4d, to the Infirmary of the Abbey his pewter dishes. His will was in great detail his possessions distributed to the occupant of the Abbey and the ones most in need within close proximity of the Abbey.

Henry Cox in the early part of the 16th century was Abbott and held his authority for 30 years. In 1534 John Fasset who together with the Canons ended the authority of the Pope and with his with eight Canons made Henry VIII supreme head of the church of England, and so began the suppression of the Abbey some two years later. On May 1534 George Gifford one of the Crowns commissioners visited Chacombe Catesby, Canons Abbey and Stewardsley and Eastley St. James Abbey. His letter to Cromwell dated May 1536 states 'The head is a quite discreet man a good husbander and loved by all'. "He begged Cromwell favour of the Abbott and advised that the king should redeem it. Together with the other Commissioners Edward Knightly, John Lane and Robert Burgoyne Giffords in substantial repair and possessing the goodliest barn ever seen for stone and timber, the poor of the town greatly releaved by this house they assured Cromwell that it would be a meritorious deed with much honour if the house was allowed to continue. These reports were not accepted or appreciated at Court, the King hinted the commissioners must have been bribed. In spite of their report of the valour of 1535 declaring a total of £5213. 17s. 2½d. The house was a lesser yearly value than £200 and within the year of the early act for suppression. John Dasset died in July 1536. John Gifford wrote to Cromwell at that date begging to see if he could obtain the Abbey Land for himself, he declared Dasset had left the house and it was likely to be suppressed. The Canons were ready and able to have for its redemptions £333. 6s. 8d. and so secured the house some respite, William Brodem was appointed Abbot elected in January 1537 and then wrote to Cromwell begging the convent seals be restored to him the seal of office was regained by him by return and in August 1538 the same year it was used in the dreaded deed of surrendering by Abbott Brohden Prior Edwards and four Canons the Abbot was rewarded with a pension of £11. 6s. 8d. the rectory of Watford and all amounting to £40 including the Rectory types of Syltesworth.

For some 100 years Cromwell commissioners, left this huge site a stoneyard where builders helped themselves. In some of the 17th century cottages in Duston, worked and decorated sandstone was found when work was carried out inside and plaster removed. St. Peters Church Tower restored in the 18th century has since been found to contain similar stone with the carved stone on the inside and thought to have come from the Abbey site. Thomas Giffard a desentant of Nicholas Giffard sold the property in 1637 to Mr. Parker. The mansion was later destroyed by fire. The Parker family are buried in Duston Church. An 1662 report, of the condition of Duston Church states that "Mr. Parkers special seat stands under the bell tower."

Abbey Church Misericord seats

On the suppression of the Abbey Nicholas Gifford did obtain the Monastic lands and built a mansion on the site of the Abbey. His son was Rector of Gayton removed six Misericord seats from the remains of the Abbey Church there beautiful carved choir oak seats depict scenes from the life of Christ. The explanation and merging of the beautiful carvings on the S.E. Misericord seats in Gayton Church as described as follows (Unfortunately the wording on the two boards above the seats in somewhat illegible these having been there many years). The inscriptions are on the south side of the chancel are:

1. Three figures in long robes seated on above. Over the central figure a mutilated object. It may represent the three persons of the Holy Trinity, or there Three Marys. On each side a crown ending in a scallop shell from which issues foliage.

2. A figure seated on a throne. Four small figures on either side issue from square apertures. It may represent the Last Judgement. On each side sunflowers and leaves.

3. A figure in a long robe has hair falling in long locks on either side of his face, seated astride a horse saddled and bridled. They pass through a rocky wood, above a demi-figure in a cape a pulpit or niche, their hands clasped together in prayer it may be an offering after a pilgrimage or journey or the representation of an incident in one of the Fabliaux on each side fruit and foliage.

On the north side of the chancel choir:-

1. A figure in a fast flowering robe fastened at the waist wearing a brooch with extended arms she holds on to the robe on either side. It may be a virgin protecting the souls of the dead.

2. A lion and dragon fighting over a small animal, perhaps the small animals is the lion's cub, the object of the dragons hate, as stated in the Bestiaries. On one side a human head cowled grotesque, fur footed and winged, on the other a dragon curled.

3. A large figured winged, his body clothed in feather, a shield on his right arm, seated astride two small human figures. Their heads in base. The dexter in a long robe, the sinster in short tunic. Their left hand and right hands are raised in the centre. The sinster holds a rosary in his left hand, they both wear flat caps. It may represent St. Michael protecting the donors of the stall. On one side an ape, on the other a kneeling figure in a tunic, buttoned before some mutilated object, a cushion behind; at his left side a hammer.

Great Seals of the early Monastic Orders of old Northampton.

Monastic floor tile found on the site of St. James Abbey.

121

TAXATIO ECCLESIASTICA P. NICHOLAI IV. A. D. 1291 (20 Edw. 1).
Abbatia S'c'i Jacobi juxta Northt.

Dioc. Linc. (Northt.)	li.	s.	d.		li.	s.	d.
Porc' in Eccl'ia de Rode"	iii	vi	viij	in Sprotten de redd'			vi
in Northt. de redd'°	iiii			in Horpol in redd'			iij
ibid' de redd' ad pitanc'	iiii			in Kiselingbur' de redd'		xi	iiij
in Dyston in t'ris, redd' et p'tis	v	xvi		in Harleston in t'ris et redd'	iiij	xviij	iiij
ibid. de redd' ad pitanc' Monachor'	iii	xviij	viii	in Villa de Flora	ij	iij	iiij
in Wotton et Abrington et le Hyde et Gerdon* in t'ris p'tis redd'	iiii	xiiij	j	in Villa de Brimpton de redd'	j	v	
in Lithebar' in t'ris"	i	iiij		in Villa de Olthrop de redd'		iij	
in Bosegate Eston Hecham et Craneford in t'ris redd' deducend'	iiij	vij	vij	in Villa de Heyford	v	iiij	vj
ibid in fruct' greg' et a'i'al'	iiij	v		in Geyton et Tyffeld in t'ris reddit' ad pitanc'		viij	viij
in West Haddon de p'tis	x			(Bed.)			
in Watford in p'tis redd' t'ris et redd' pastur'�q	vi	xv		in Newenh'm de redd'ʳ		vij	xj
ibid in fruct' greg' et a'i'al'	xij	x		in Turveye de redd'	ij	vj	viij
in Brochole de redd' ad pitanc'	iij			in Harewolde in t'ris redd' et pastur'	j		
in Billing de redd' et mol'	ij	xvi		(Rutl.) in Decan' Rotel'ˢ			iiij
in Brampton in t'ris	x			(Leic.) in Decan' Gosecoteᵗ			viij
				(Summa lxx li. ijd.)			

VALOR ECCLESIASTICUS, temp. Hen. VIII.

[Abstract of Return 26 Hen. 8 (1535). First Fruits Office.]

Abb'ia S'c'i Jacobi juxᴬ Northampton'.
Joh'nes Bassett ✝ Abbas incumbens ib'm.

Valet in Temporal'
Scit' Abb'ie cum Terr' D'nical'.

Exit' & pfic' omn' ortoȝ gardinaȝ grovett' aquaȝ piscar' infra scitum abbie ad xlviii s. p annū ac terr' p'toȝ pasc' & pastur' dnicaliū ad xi li. ij s. p annū simull in man' & occupac' ipius abbis & convent' ejusdm nunq'm p'ris arrentat' & modo tᵃm p vic' inquis' & scrutac' tᵃm dictoȝ cōmissionar' qᵃm p xᶜᵉᵐ homin' jurat' valuat' viz. ad sumam   } xiij x

Reddit' in com' North'mp'
Reddit' & firm' in divs' man⁹iis villis & hamlett' in com' North'mpton p annū.

	li.	s.	d.
In North'mpton'	xxxviij	xvij	
Flower		lv	vijob.
Ferthingston	xiij	iiij	
Kyslingbury	vij	ij	
Wotton	xij		
Bylling	xvij		
Gaddisdén [Herts]	xiij	iiij	
Hangynghoughton	vij		
Kelmshe	ij	vij	
Holcot	vij	viij	
West Haddon	iij		
Bructon		xij	
Wold	ij	ix	
Stavton	iij		
Stokbruerne	xij		
Bosynhoo molendin'	iij		
Grenden	iij		
Spratton	xl		
Ritherthropp	x		
Houghton m'	xij		
Cotton Marshe	xxxv	iiij	
Wekley	lxvj	viij	

cxxxi vij ij ob.

		li.	s.	d.	a
In Harleston	-	vi	v	ij	
Patishull	-	xij	xviij	viij	
Dalyngton	-'	xx			
Bukby	-	xiiij			
Duston	-	viij	xij		
Vico Sc̄e Jacobi	vij	viij			
Colingtre	-	xvij			
Middelton	-	xlj	iiij		

Redd' in Lundon'
Reddit' in Charingcross' in suburb' Lundon' p annū   } xl

Nundin' S'c'i Jacobi.
D' aliquo pfic' pvenien' de nundin' tent' in die Sc̄i Jacobi annuati non r' p eo qᵈ nullū pfic' inde pvenit ultra cust' & expenc' in & sirca easdm eodm die fact' sup serm dc̄i abbis et ⁊o hic   } nˡ

cxlvj li. xvij s. ij ob.

SP'R'UAL'
Rector' cum Penc'
Firm' rector' vicar' cum penc' in divs' villis in com' North'mpton' p annū viz.

	i.	s.	d.
Rector' de Wekley	cvj	viij	
Firm' rector' de Sprotton	} xiiij		
Firm' rector' de Wodford ✝ & Silleswo'the	} xxviij	xij	iiij
Firm' rector' de Horton	} lx		lxvij
Rector' de Thropp	lx		
Decim' in Hyde	iiij		

List of income of rents and taxes due to St. James Abbey for 1291 and before its dissolution of 1538.

Franklin Gardens

These gardens were built by John Collier founder of the large boot and shoe works in St. James. Simon Collier his brother greatly enlarged these works in Harlestone Road finding employment for hundreds of people in St. James before the first war to 1935.

In 1865 he brought a new era to Northampton working class, a recreational area was established, well laid out gardens with large heated glasshouses, 11 acres of attractively laid out flower gardens, with conservatories on the south wall, a large ornamental lake, cricket ground, running and cycle track, dancing pavilion, band stand and tea rooms. The gardeners houses on the extreme end of the property has a plaque, high on the front "Melbourne Place" now a listed property, on the whole a remarkable enterprise for its time and a tribute to Queen Victoria's first Prime Minister the owner of Duston manor the second Lord Melbourne.

Saturday May 27th 1865 was the day Melbourne Gardens were first open to the public by Lord Burghley. The "Mercury" recalls under the distinguished patronage of Lord Burghley the band of the Northamptonshire Militia will perform in the gardens during the day. All proceeds on the opening day will be given to Northampton Infirmary. Admission 6d all Soldiers and Volunteers in uniform half price. Open 10 a.m. in the morning.

Here are some of the other attractions advertised in the local "Herald" in the days of Melbourne Gardens. Monster Display of Fireworks at Duston. Monday August 2nd on a scale of Crystal Place magnificence, Admission One Shilling, after 6 p.m. 6d.

Monday September 6th 1869. Under the patronage of Her Majesty's 4th Regiment of Foot Weedon Depot Assault of Arms – Athletic Sports – Ascent of six Balloons – Balloon Race – Ascent of a Monster Magnesium Balloon. Admission 1/-, after 4 p.m. 6d.

Monday August 9th 1869 Grand Velocipede Tournament. First bicycle races will take place. Open to all England. Entrance Fee 5/- First Prize Silver Cup. Second races open to residents of Northampton. First Prize Silver Cup. Both races to be run in one mile heats, for the people fashionable place of resort. One of the best racing grounds in the Midlands. Admission 6d Children 3d. Melbourne Gardens open every day throughout the season. The band of the Fifth N.R.V. (Northampton Rifle Volunteers) in attendance for dancing on Monday and Saturday.

John Collier like his father was a town councillor in various aspects of town affairs, chairman of the early Tramway Company, the Northampton Board of Guardians, the Duston School Board and Hardingstone Local Board. He died on May 2nd 1885 and is buried in a brick grave in the old Northampton General Cemetery, he was 62. His home was the Cendars, Weedon Road. Mr. Upton is shown as the next proprietor. By 1880 Mr. J. C. Franklin who owned a large hotel in Guildhall Road announced his latest acquisition of the Pleasure Gardens, Duston Road with continuous attraction all the year round. Season tickets 10/-.

Jubilee Hall, Franklins Gardens

Upon the death of John Collier, Mr. John Franklin purchased The Gardens and promptly enlarged them into one of the most attractive venues of entertainments in the Midlands. Special train trips were laid on for the day and 20,000 people are reported to be there on a bank holiday. Apart from owning Franklins Hotel in Guildhall Road which started as Franklins Restaurant he also built the Opera House now the Royal Theatre in conjunction with his friend Mr. Isaac Tarry. His first project at the gardens was to build the Jubilee Hall, he saw the need for all the year round pleasure and quickly made the interior as follows:

The Great Jubilee Hall is furnished with a new and excellently-appointed stage which will be admirably adapted for Concerts, Vaudevilles, or Operettas. The proscenium is composed of six Corinthian pillars, the shafts painted in porphyry, the capitals in gilt; Between them hang painted draperies of Venetian damask. Flanking each side of the stage are statues of Bacchus, and Arladne on malachite pedestals. The act-drop which is very artistically painted, represents the Lake of Come. At present there is but one scene, representing a drawing-room, the scheme of colours of which is in primrose and French grey. Through the wide central widows a view is gained of a path in an Italian landscape, with a fountain at the extreme end.

To the dressing-rooms included in the original plan, two new ones have been added. The Jubilee Hall may now certainly claim to be one of the largest, prettiest and best appointed in the Midlands.

Indeed the people of the town ought to feel proud that they have such a splendid pleasure resort to fall back upon during the dull winter months. That end of the large hall which was formerly occupied by the stage and proscenium has given place to a representation of a large cavern of rock, through the centre of which, arches and grottoes of coral ore seem to rise, cleverly modelled swans and aquatic plants, and in the background the setting sun appears to be just sinking below the horizon. So ingenious are the lighting arrangements, that the appearance of the cavern can be either extended or contracted. Looked at from the opposite end of the hall, the appearance of the cavern is really very effective, and quite a triumph of the scenic painters art. The wall at the reverse end of the hall has been painted to represent a woodland scene. Along one side of the hall are imitation palm trees some 18 feet high, which have a very good effect. The leaves are ingeniously cast in metal, and painted to represent the original as nearly as possible. Baskets of flowers are suspended from the girders of the roof, and these together with several pieces of statuary and shrubs, combine to make the hall what it has been so well described, as the "Palace of Flora."

Football at Franklins

Simon Collier the boot Manufacturer combined to help John Franklin, as he helped his founder brother John Collier and in 1886 they decided to call a meeting in the Melbourne Tavern to all concerned with football in Northampton to discuss and put into shape the necessary arrangements to promote Football in the Gardens – Quote:

"The liberal idea of giving a County Champion Cup valued at £20 ought to rouse action in the breast of every team in Northampton. We hope to see a large attendance of the local clubs and their patrons and this important matter put into working order. Meanwhile we can only remark that it is the best and most expensive prize that has been offered for football and may the best man win it!"

Sale of Franklin's Gardens 1888

In 1888 all John Colliers properties including the Gardens were put up for sale. The Opera House, Franklin Hotel Restaurant, The Swan Hotel and the Dolphin Hotel, extract from the sale report: "The sale was conducted by Messrs. Macquire and Tarry experts in the sale of licensed properties, yesterday there was a whole battalion present. The sale took place in the large and handsome Assembly Room of the George Hotel, Northampton there were several Brewers and Hotel keepers there, a good number of Solicitors etc. A few minutes before four o' clock Mr. Pickering Phipps entered the room followed by his son and Councillor T. Phipps Dorman, Councillor Ratliffe (Ratliffe and Jeffery). Mr. Isaac Tarry friend of John Franklin was the Auctioneer. The sale was somewhat spoiled of its interest as the main property Franklins Gardens was sold privately prior to the sale to Messrs. Pugh and Phillips for the sum of £17,000.

This is a compact and valuable property in Guildhall Road. A portion of the stabling of the Swan Hotel was included in the lot, thus joining the Hotel to the Opera House at the Cow Lane End, with the Swan Hotel. It has a frontage in Guildhall Road of 65½ft. It is a handsome looking building, and it does an immense trade. It was built from designs of the late Mr. E. F. Law: it is of Gothic character: and its front being only two doors from the Opera House it is largely patronised by theatre-goers. Besides that, a very large wine and spirit trade, both wholesale and retail, has been done. It is famous as a restaurant, and the catering has always been regarded as first class. It has 18 bedrooms. The additional piece of land included in the lot would enable 20 additional bed and sitting-rooms to be erected, and a billiard-room all of which would be a paying addition to the premises. The property has an area of about 6,650 square feet, and according to the Auctioneer it had cost Mr. Franklin some £8,000. The bidding was started at £7,000. Immediately there were two bids at £7,500. The next offer was £8,000. Very rapidly additional bids of £100 each were offered, and in four minutes from the start, the property was knocked down to Mr. Pickering Phipps, for Messrs. P. Phipps and Co. Limited for £8,500.

The Swan Hotel (1888 sale)

The next lot to be offered was the Swan Hotel, a very large property in Derngate and Cow Lane. It is one of the oldest licensed houses in Northampton, and during the last century it has done a large and prosperous business. Since the Theatre has been opened it has also obtained a large share of theatrical custom. Five years ago the property was almost entirely re-built from the designs of Mr. C. Dorman. It covers 4,300 feet and is in the occupation of Mr. W.D. Manning. The first bid was for £2,500. With a rush £600-£700-£800-£900 and £3,000 were offered in succession. This last bid, it is understood was made by Mr. Pickering Phipps. Then there was a lull. £100 was called out by a gentleman near Mr. Tarry: Mr. Pickering Phipps nodded his head: the Auctioneer said going! going! gone! and Mr. Pickering Phipps was loudly applauded on being the purchaser for his company of the property at £3,200.

The Dolphin (1888 sale)

The Dolphin Hotel in Gold Street was the next property. Some little interest was centred in this because it was well known that Mr. Franklin bought it by public auction only a year or so ago: and that he gave only £4,300 for it: It is an old place rather, and was really the sporting lot of the sale. It ought to be pulled down and re-built. Mr. Franklin says he had that intention at one time. It occupies one of the best, if not the best, position in the whole town for a grand Hotel: and a short time ago there were suggestions that a better site could nowhere be found than the Dolphin for a covered market, having as it has, a good frontage in Gold Street and a long frontage on two thoroughfares in Kingswell Street. It is a compact property and covers an area of nearly 14,000 square feet.

Amusements for the new owner

A managerial report 1889 shows vast improvements, the complex had grown from eleven acres to 30 acres with stands huge planting of shrubs on a site called Abbey Park (now Express Lift) extracts from the report of the Mercury of 1889 as follows:

Franklin Gardens since the absorption of Abbey Park into them have not been fully described, so that a brief summary of the improvements effected under the new regime, will we venture to think, be acceptable to our readers. The most notable feature of the place is the new race course which has a run of nearly a mile, and an average width of 50 feet. One of its chief advantages is that people in the enclosure of the Grand Stand will be able to witness the race from start to finish. All the accessories of places of this description, such as saddling paddocks, judge's boxes, and weighing and dressing-rooms, will not be wanting, and although much remains to be done, yet it is confidently believed that everything will be in readiness by the first Meeting which is fixed for the 24th inst.

Unquestionably the work next in point of importance, is the bicycle track now in course of formation, and which encircles the new cricket ground. With 3 3/4 laps to the mile, and a straight run home of 140 yards, it is intended that this track shall be one of the fastest in England. Thousands of loads of stone and rubble have been hand-pitched into the bottom of it.

Pursuing our way westward, we notice a pretty pond belted with pink hawthorn, Portugal laurels and mountain ash, whilst hard by is a swimming tank 8 feet deep, which will be utilized on fete days for feats of notation. The object which will perhaps excite most admiration is the lake, now indeed worthy of the name, being some two acres in extent, and dotted with seven islets. The portion added by the new company are ornamented with grand and stately old trees, the lack of which was so painfully evident in the original grounds. The directors evidently keenly appreciate the value which timber has in investing pleasure gardens with a delightfully rural look, and so have wisely added to the fine old elms and oak and ash which they found there by plantations of youngling, walnut, aspen, beech, larch, chestnut, hawthorn, lime, hazel, laburnum and Lombardy poplars. Altogether, we understand, nearly 3,000 flowering trees and shrubs have already been planted, and the work still goes on. Any notice of the Gardens which contained no reference to the new bear pit would be indeed incomplete. This is 70 foot long, and is provided with picturesque rock and stone stage or platforms. The Monkey House is vastly improved by a better system of lighting, and new pigeon and dove cotes have been erected. A fine scenoscopic gallery which will be illuminated day and night on fete days, will be one of the permanent attractions of the place to which are now being added, by Messrs. Allchin, Linnell: and Co., a number of their new patented steam roundabouts, sway-boats, and a pair of the largest aerial cars in England. A new committee-room for use for athletic sports, has been built in the form of a miniature Swiss chalet. Certainly Franklin's Gardens and Abbey Park would be a credit to cities of ten times our population, and the whole town and county may justly feel proud of the possession of a place large enough for any open-air function, no matter on what scale. That it supplies to a great public that the company will receive an adequate return for their great outlay, pluck and enterprise is earnestly to be hoped. Franklin's Gardens are to Northampton what the Crystal Palace is to a larger public, and will doubles receive as much support from the shire as from the borough. Justly the Manager claims that it is suitable to almost every form of English games, pastimes and recreation – cricket, tennis, rackets, football, golf, pole, lacrosse, quoits, bowls, races, cycling, swimming, skating, curling, archery, hurling, hockey and steeplechases.

Various questions were asked by the Mercury newspapers reporter regarding the proposed pony and race and meetings. Meetings were registered with the Jockey Club and National Hunt Committee four on the flat and two over the hurdles. The grounds will be enclosed with corrugated iron, eight feet high inside which will be shrubs etc., to relieve the monotonous appearance. Will you erect stands? yes, and where will you build them? Opposite the Red House and the winning post. What will be the name of your meeting? "Abbey Park" Why Abbey Park? because the new part taken in is known as the Abbey Lands and arrangements can be made to carry on the meeting quite independent of the Gardens by putting up a fence. What is the present share capital of your new company? £25,000 and if the whole should prove a failure the land will be worth the money. (Northampton Mercury 1880-1888)

Franklins Gardens, the name is now synonymous with Rugby Football and has been the home of the Saints for over 60 years. An exciting time in our St. James School days was the afternoons off to go to see the East Midlands at the Gardens with the huge crowds. I remember counting eleven trams in line waiting for the end of the match. The last one, the first to return, filled to capacity, the conductor took the fares as they got off.

1937

Franklins Gardens Tennis Courts

Cedos Motorcycles of St. James

Mr. Martin Smith a friend of mine and proud owner of one of the original St. James made Cedos Motorcycles has passed on to me this unique history from the former owner and enthusiast Mr. P. Staughton. The commencement of production began in Westbridge Works in 1926 under the name of Cedos Motorcycles Ltd., from the start of the company it would appear they made a useful range of machines details as follows for the enthusiast:

21/2 hp (67x20) 247cc single speed, belt drive, two stroke engine, 24x12/4 wheels.
21/2 hp (67x70) 247cc two stroke engine, Sturmey Archer 3 speed gearbox, chain cum belt drive, 24x21/4 wheels and tyres. 23/4 hp (71x88) 350cc four stroke engine, Sturmey Archer 3 speed gearbox, all chain drive, 26x3 wheels, hand change with kick start.

Here is a list of the frame nos. found below the saddle.

1920 001 – 600 1921 600 – 1300 1922/23 and 1924 1300 – 3,600 1925 to Sept 1927 3,600 – 7523

By 1927 the range of machines changed very little, there were still two 250cc two strokes and two 300cc four strokes, all models using Sturmey Archer gearbox and all using chain drive. Some Cedos models were available in 1929, these were 147, 172 and 247cc two strokes. No factory production can be shown after late 1927. Models on sale after 1927 must have been the remnants of stock left when the factory closed.

Cedos Engineering Companies continued to operate at Westbridge from the closing of the Motorcycle works continuing through the last war until 1980 when the last company was acquired by Servais Silencers who moved the entire stock of machinery to their new premises on Harlestone Road, New Duston. The old site is now part of Travis Timber Yard.

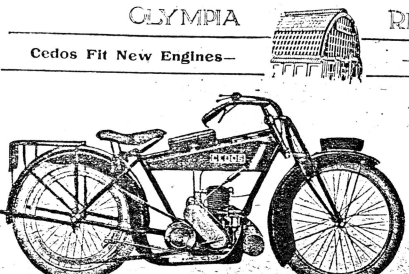

OLYMPIA REPORT

Cedos Fit New Engines— —Chater Lea Features.

The Cedos is a two-stroke which particularly impressed us during a recent road test.

The bare running expenses, apart from insurance, depreciation, and driver's wages are considered to be 2d. per mile. The company's 2¼ h.p., 2¾ h.p., 3½ h.p., 6 h.p., and 8 h.p. machines, though being made as usual, are not being exhibited.

and of the constant mesh type. It is circular in form and is enclosed in a special lug forming part of the frame. and a cubic capacity of 211 c.c. The gearbox is the Cedos plain two-speed, The usual Cedos spring fork is fitted, and the top tube of the frame slopes down throughout its length from the head to the seat pillar tube, giving, in conjunction with the 24 in. wheels, an exceptionally low riding position. The top tube of the lady's model leaves the head at the same angle as that on the gent.'s, but after a few inches it drops down at an angle of about 45 degrees with the horizontal, until it meets the down tube about midway between the saddle and the gearbox. The prices of these models are 70 guineas for the gent.'s and 72 guineas for the lady's machines.

The two new types shown are a two-speed Sporting model gentleman's solo motorcycle, and a two-speed lady's side-carette. The engine on both of them is of quite new design. It is the two-stroke type with transfer passage through the piston, and has a detachable cylinder head held on to the body of the

1927 Cedos Motorcycles

Dover Ltd

We still recall the landmark of St. James, Northampton of the imposing 130ft chimney with Dover Ltd. in bold lettering facing the town and festooned encased with Virginia Creeper climbing almost to the top, but for the furnace smoke, planted by its founder of the firm Mr. H.W. Dover in 1920. A remarkable engineer he came to Northampton and commenced building in Park Road, St. James opposite the Castle Inn. In 1897 after being educated at Birkbeck Engineering Institute, London he passed on to Messrs. Chipperfield & Co. London model making engineers and stayed for 13 years helping making working models for international exhibitions all over the world. This experience was to help him later in his own export business. In his lifetime he had over a hundred inventions patented enabling the firm to expand and grow. Initially perhaps his most important invention, the Dover Detachable Gear Case, kept the 150 workpeople fully engaged in the earlier years. It had a world wide appeal, no longer would the ladies long dresses get covered with chain oil gentleman 'could ride their cycles in their Sunday suits, the "Hercules" in the late 1920's was £2.19.6d and I remember and another £1 extra for a three speed gear. His invention "Exonite" which we all thought of as Celluloid was a much harder compound described as "This most hard substance can be manufactured into McFalliferons articles of utility and ornament. I remember the show case displays of gear cases, chain covers, mud guards, intubular covering cycle clips, handle bar covers, steering wheel covers etc.

While at Messrs. Chipperfields Mr. Dover noticed at the railway stations the childrens pennies not being returned from "Nestles" Chocolate machines, when the machines were empty, so he promptly invented a method of returning coins. Although there was a narrow viewing slit in the machine to see the flat chocolate pack in its red wrappings the thick continuous grime covered the entire slot machine.

Ping Pong popular at the turn of the century resulted in the firm making these balls in huge lead quantities, suddenly the craze collapsed, left with a huge stock, his inventiveness lead to making a toy cannon which he named the "Woolwich Infant" 16" long which fired the Ping Pong balls which eventually depleted the stock. Today table tennis its successor has its world wide appeal and international teams and players. In 1908 a fire devastated the works so much inflammable material was involved that the damage was estimated at £15,000 Mr. Ron Ward who I am indebted for the detail of Messrs. Dover was a member of the staff as was his father Fred Ward who began work there in 1903. Ron has a photograph of his grandfather an auxiliary fireman standing in the burnt out factory. A family continuation of service of three generations. W. Dover built a large hall on the corner of Park Road and West Bridge for roller skating a craze before the 1914-18 War, later to be opened as St. James Cinema always known to us boys as the "Rink", two shows a week 2d for children on Saturday afternoons. Mr. Tyrell "Buck" was the uniformed attendant, a man of ample proportions, the official thrower out, he would check each boy coming in as the long queue down Park Road entered "You lot are not coming in", He said on fronting a gang, he had trouble with, I reckon it was you lot that ripped the seats last week. So hot was it in there on a Summers afternoon with the corrugated iron roof and only a wooden shutter high up on either side of the building operated by "Buck" with a long rope that supplied what little air there was, our faces were so wreathed in sweat it was difficult to see the screen. Peanut shells and empty bottles made a a hazardous and noisy approach in the dark to anyone leaving to get an icecream. Everything was thrown at the pianist on the stage heavily playing it to accompany the "rescuing" cowboy films.

Mr. Dover's inventions were astounding, his "Doverite", a non inflammable material was used and acclaimed by Kay Don, 1931 his "Silver Bullet" record breaking world speed car and by Donald Campbell in "Bluebird" in 1929 for the inclusion of the special steering wheels. This was also used for over-head handrails for passengers moving along a crowded bus, also for covering the alighting and boarding bar on the step of the bus, all these consisted of a twisted grip in the material. On March 4th, 1933 he opened the Dover Hall between the Cinema and the Works, this addition was completed with the entire floor lain in Canadian Maple. Also to complete his leisure enterprises he provided a Gymnasium between the Cinema on St. James Road and Whittons the "last" manufacturers. He died in April 1933, he not only brought added employment to St. James but pleasure too. He was a town councillor for many years, Mayor in 1925 and Alderman of the Borough for the remainder of his years. His wife was also honoured for her work during the 1914-18 War with the M.B.E. She continued to live in the house he built for many years afterwards "Holyrood House", Harlestone Road. At his funeral the County Amateur Athletic Club Members acted as his pallbearers in recognition of his interest and provision of their headquarters in the Gymnasium.

In 1955 the works were taken over by Bluemels, by then the Roxy Cinema, Gymnasium and Dance Hall were closed and in 1970 the whole of the old Dover land disposed of. Today stands the Dover Court sheltered housing complex.

St. James Church

St. James Church was being built in 1868 at a cost of £3,000, the need for this arose from the Industrial Boot and Shoe Expansion and the extensive new housing extending West from Northampton. The Amalgamation of Duston and Dallington parishes from all the land then in that area resulted in 1872 a new district parish of the town. At the Churches completion a commemorative tablet containing the coat of arms of the Thornton family was placed in the Church and reads as follows: "Placed as a mark of great respect and appreciation for the encouragement and help given by Rev. William Thornton and his descendants at the time that this parish was formed and the church was built, in 1870". (Brockhall was the residence of the Thornton Family for 350 years. 1920 saw the addition of the high clock tower, most people at work or at home can still look up for the time visible from one of its four clock faces and it was built by generous contributions from all in the parish including Congregational and Methodist Churches as a monument to those who lost their lives in the first War.

The tower clock was given by the late Mr. & Mrs. J. Grose (The Coachbuilders) of St. James in memory of their son Albert George (Lieut. 1914-18). It was first placed in a lower part of the tower and could not be seen by the Grose's and others of the Churches benefactors who lived on the Western part of St. James so it was raised to its present height.

Coming to school one morning a crowd had gathered outside the church to see the large weather cock that had been blown down off the tower, it was never replaced. The extremely fine organ was installed in 1913 at a cost of £700 by Brindley and Foster. This was made possible by the generous gift of £350 by Andrew Carnegie Trust.

The peal of bells were given by Mr. & Mrs. W. L. Green as a thanks offering. These tubular bells provide the striking notes for the clock ringing out the quarters.

Before the War we used to listen intently in the evenings to the members of the Church playing hymns on them. Invariably as they practised the notes on the bells there would be a pause after the wrong note had been played they would begin again and again, the same hymn. This form of bell playing seems to have gone out of fashion and the iron frame and wires removed from most Churches. When the Church was extended in 1890 the pulpit was left incomplete, three extra pillars were added to match the original ones. This decorative stone and brick pulpit is in complete harmony with the building in design, and Victorian architecture. The completion of it was donated by Mr. A.E. Smith, an active member of St. James Church at that time, to the memory of his parents, William Samuel Smith and Louise Smith (who kept the Butchers Shop and Slaughter House opp the "Green Man" in St. James Road, father and son business for some 60 years. A.E. Smith retired from his Butchers and Market Garden activities after the last War, and in 1946 we brought the site in Millway from him for Nurseries now the Garden Centre.

1905 saw the completion of the Church Institute in Spencer Bridge Road adjacent to Dallington Mill. The site was given by Rt. Hon. Charles Robert Spencer of Dallington who later succeeded to the Earldom at Althorpe after the death of Margaret his wife he gave Dallington Hall to Northampton Corporation in memory of her, it is worth recalling that all that East Side of Harlestone Road and St. James Road to West Bridge was Spencer property hence Althorpe Road, Sunderland Street, Countess Road. The foundation stone of the Institute was laid by Lady Knightley of Fawsley. Now a section of the Church provides facilities for the many other church activities, the old hall which was always a distance away from the main worship has now been disposed of. In 1921 a beautiful screen was erected in the church designed in early style, again the work of the Duston Architect George Stevenson was given by Mr. A.E. Marlow (Boot and Shoe Manufacturer, their factory then in Vicarage Road, St. James still bears the elaborate Datestone – St. James Works 1907), and was given in memory of their Son Lieutenant Stanley Marlow who was killed 1914-18.

St. James Church has a reputation for its uniformed youth organisations, such as the guides, brownies, scouts, cubs and their junior sections, but longest serving of all is the church lads brigade. The St. James Company was formed as long ago as 16th June, 1900 and been in existence continually ever since, its members serving the church in many ways. It has had many long serving officers over the years, Len Hurst, Reg Dolman, Percy Robinson and his sons Jack, Frank and Ray, Arthur Chaplen, Ron Warren, David Harris later to become

National Assistant General Secretary David Feetham, John Oxborough and so on. Of these gentlemen, Reg, Arthur and Ron went on to become Battalion Commanders of the Peterborough Diocesan Battalion of which the company is part.

In later years the Brigade merged with the Church Girls Brigade, and the organisation is now known as the Church Lads and Church Girls Brigade. The present company commander is Louise Craddock.

In 1950, at the celebrations of the companies Golden Jubilee, an ex. members association was formed to assist the company where possible, and a Reunion and Supper has been held annually ever since.

Memorial plaque placed in St. James Church for the appreciation of the Thornton family who helped found the church who lived at Thornton Park, Kingsthorpe.

1889

St. James Church

1960

Diamond Jubilee Parade of St. James Church Lads Brigade leaving Church.

1959

Monthly Parade of St. James Church Lads Brigade leaving Church.

St. James Church tower has overlooked great changes for almost a hundred years.

1866

Before St. James Church was built. This early part of the School was used for worship.

1917

A plaque to the memory of 2 girls who were killed in a Zeppelin Air Raid is in the Girls' Department.

1960

The old toll house built at the Old Turnpike Road to Dallington Village off Spencer Bridge Rd. was used by St. James Church as the caretaker's house for their Institute. (Now demolished)

St. James School

The story of St. James Church of England National School began in 1866 although most of the dwellings were in the old area near Westbridge and Mill Road. Streets did not appear till 1876 when Alma Street and Devonshire Street were being built, before 1866 children walked to their old parish school at Duston (built 1856) so few children attended when it was opened, only 25. Here are some of the details of the first weekly attendances at St. James

May
29th Tuesday Discovered that the lower section was very backward indeed in scripture.
30th Wednesday Taught the boys the evening hymns.
31st Thursday Cautioned the boys about scratching the desks and leaving the playground at playtime.

June
19th Tuesday Had to punish several boys misbehaving during prayers.
20th Wednesday Two ladies visiting the school were surprised to find so many present.
21st Thursday A great number of boys late in the afternoon.
22nd Friday Cautioned the boys about going into the hayfield.
By the autumn of 1866 some 50 more pupils were admitted

August
24th Tuesday A boy who was sent to school played truant and went gleaning instead.
25th Wednesday Punished several boys in the morning for coming with rough heads, and most boys came with smooth hair in the afternoon.

September
6th Monday At 3.00 a boy was brought to school by his mother, he had been kept away to glean and so got to rather dislike school by laying a thick stick on his shoulders occasionally.
17th Friday Several scholars absent. They went to see Mander's menagerie, which arrived today.
20th Monday Northampton Cheese Fair. Apart from many scholars absent on account of it in the afternoon. Only about 25 present and some of those went out before time.
21st Tuesday 72 Scholars were present in the morning.
1867 Childrens sickness in the winter months often due to cold classrooms made the teachers task then more difficult than in the Summer Months problems with outdoor tasks of parents haymaking, harvesting not making them attend school.

1867 Now 96 Scholars in the small first part of the school now full, by 1894 as the population grew in the now St. James Parish accommodation was provided for 180 girls and 225 infants and 250 boys. The infant block with its entrance at the jitty back of Althorpe Road and in 1898 an extra Junior Extension for another 103. By Autumn of 1898
2nd September The attendance has been a little better this week. There are several boys away in the corn fields gleaning. Boys have been taken away from the school owing to the strong feeling in the District during the late school board election.
17th September "Distribution of the Aid Grant submitted by the Governing Body of the above Association under section 1 (4), of the voluntary schools act, has been approved by this department, and that in accordance there with a grant of £217.7.2. will be paid as soon as possible to the London Agent of the bank at which the school account is kept.

This grant is made for the purpose of maintaining improved staff (£132.7.2), increased salaries (£25), and providing new desks and apparatus (£60), and my lords will be required to be satisfied that it has been expended".

In the 1920s I remember the unaltered East to West original long 1966 building divided into four classrooms with the Masters (room in the centre), this building was first used for Church Worship the altar being in the East End then the girls department until St. James Church was built.

October 19th 1917
In the 1914-18 war during a Zeppelin raid two sisters were killed. A plaque commemorating them Glady's and Lillian Gammons was placed on the wall of their classroom. My own recollection of the boys dept. are of satisfaction in learning the three 'R's. Punishment to fit the crime of the boys and a respect of our teachers

and elders. The cane was the cure for any diversions. The range in the masters cupboard was awesome were selected accordingly three foot to four foot tested first in one of two swishes in the air all in front of the class. In each class was one tortoise stove which the teacher never left in cold weather and in a severe spell we all would be sent home.

St. James Day and All Saints day began with all children attending Church then home. When National Schools began the Church of England constituted the Vicar or Rector as Chairman. St. James with its boot and shoe expansion at the turn of the century produced rows of Coronation type houses, day school and Sunday schools were overflowing with children, large families spilled out into the streets and parks on summer evening. Some 10 years ago I met Rev. Harold Brinkley minister of Doddridge Memorial, in the late 1920's. Together we talked about the full places of worship in the 1920's how there were 1,000 Sunday School children then at Doddridge Memorial he remarked you would find 100 children playing next door in Marlborough Road after day school. Corporal punishment was the order of the day, fighting, scrumping apples and bad language was all dealt with the cane on both hands, other parts of the anatomy were caned for serious offences usually by the head master. In severe weather we would all be sent home a tortoise stove in the centre of each classroom was the only source of heat and the teacher would almost sit on that all day. Anyone spotted chewing half penny liquorice sticks or spearmint or if they dare suck a 1d gobstopper the stove door would be opened and the offending sweet was spat in.

Absenteeism continued in the schools every year, when all the family went to Northampton Races or St. George's Fairs held on the Market Square, or Duston Feast held at New Duston also in celebrations later to mark the end of the Boar War.

By the turn of the century discipline was still a problem and was not easy to apply. Irate parents would attack teachers who had dealt severely with a boy for stealing or swearing and the local bobby led the parents away to be dealt with by the local court. Over the years the teachers tasks became more rewarding and improved reports far more satisfactory regarding the curriculum. 1936 St. James school had their first meeting with Spencer School where the older group of children would be transferred.

January 21st 1936 A short address was given to the children this morning on the occasion of the death of our own beloved King George V and the abdication of King Edward VIII the National Anthem was sung as a prayer.

February 13th A staff meeting was held today and a discussion took place on Speech Training, following the Sectional meeting of H.T.s. when a special "drive" to improve speech was suggested.

1941
The difficult years of 1939-45 War
January 23rd There is a thick fog and the light is so bad that only oral work can be taken this morning
January 31st The shelters have been too wet (1 and a half inches of water) again, this week. The matter has again been reported and a man was sent. Unfortunately every time there is a heavy or medium rain storm from 1 to 2 inches the water gets in to the shelters. This is too much to stand in. During the present snow 3" of water stood in one shelter.
February 4th Staff meeting to rearrange shelter drill.
February 12th This part of scholarship of the boys Dept. are borrowing some large room. The H.T. will take as many children as possible in the staff room and the others will work in class 3 room taking reading and oral subjects. We can take P.T. this morning as the play ground is too wet.
February 18th 27 children sent to Spencer School for the second immunisation at 11.15 this morning.

Education Controversy by the late 19th century loomed large in local and National politics. Its active alliance with liberalism in St. James large employers of labour in the community were determined to get an alternative method to the Church of England at St. James so the Education liege was established in 1898 most of its workers established from Harlestone Road Primitive Methodist and Doddridge Memorial Chapels representatives were appointed on a committee to deal with religious teaching to be provided at temporary accommodation at St. James Hall on the Square. An alternative was to sent the children to a choice of Board Schools in the town, an Infant School was established and a teacher appointed in St. James. All this alternative teaching required morning and apart from considerable help from J.D. Lewis subscriptions were required. All their efforts came to fruition with the building of a temporary Board School in St. James near to the tram sheds.

The "Tin School opened on St. James Road, April 3rd 1905 to accommodate 500 pupils, 250 mixed girls and boys and 25 infants here are some of the first entries in the attendance book.

Opening of St. James Road Council School

April 3rd The above School was opened today. 192 children were admitted. Managers meeting
April 4th 7 Children were admitted today making a total of 199 on the books of these 195 were in, in the afternoon
The timetable was received today, it was signed by His Majesty's Inspector
April 5th 1 child was admitted today making a total of 200 on the books.

1905

I am directed to inform you that the above School has been placed on the Annual Grant List as from 3rd April 1905 as a Council School.

The school year will end on the last day of October and a grant will therefore be payable, provided that the conditions of the Code are satisfied, for the period ending on that day in 1905. The School number will be 5943 and it is requested that this, together with the name of the Local Education Authority may be quoted in all official communication.

1911

A serious drawback to the efficiency of the School is the excessive temperature of the rooms in hot weather. A visit paid in the beginning of June last year a temperature of 85 and a half degrees was noted and at the end of May this year the thermometer stood at 84 degrees. It is said to have reached 90 degrees on one occasion. Even at this early period of the summer time the heat of the corrugated iron plates which faces the outside wall is almost unbearable to the hand.

The older scholars are interested in nature lessons. Some valuable experiments are being carried out in the School. Further efforts are needed to train the scholars in the upper classes to the more self reliant and in the lower part of the School to develop the powers of observation and speech. Simultaneous work should be discontinued.

1912

A senior class, St. James C. of E. Girls' School.

The History of Doddridge Memorial Congregational Church, Northampton

A commemorative tablet in Doddridge Memorial Church suggests that the centenary year of the Congregational Sunday School in St. James' End, Northampton, was 1929, but the earliest records which have been discovered occur at the beginning of 1830. At the outset, I think that it is worth while trying to visualise something of the social and religious atmosphere of the time and place.

1830 was a year of general agricultural depression, and of local industrial setbacks, with the accompanying evil of poverty and crime stalking the land. A perusal of the yellowing files of the *Northampton Mercury* provides many illuminating pictures of the prevalent social conditions. In the issue of March 5th, 1830, thirty-nine charges are reported at the assizes, mostly cases of larceny, resulting in eleven judgments of death. For example, Thoams Robinson, aged twenty, and William Pearse, aged nineteen, charged with stealing "three spoons and a large quantity of halfpence at Harpole", were sentenced to death: a man aged sixty-six who stole an article worth four shillings, was transported for life: in another case the theft of a fork earned the same drastic penalty. Such an arbitrary code of justice, which could deal out capital punishment for minor as well as major offences, encouraged rather than mitigated recklessness in crime, it seems incredible that human lives could be equated with "three spoons and a large quantity of halfpence" but it was so.

The industrial revolution had already clouded and begrimed the landscape and the life of much of Northern England and some parts of the Midlands, but Northampton's old-established staple trade, the making of boots and shoes, was indeed fortunate, in that in essence a domestic industry for several decades after 1830, so that the introduction of machinery was delayed until a more enlightened era. Nevertheless, the spirit of industrial expansion was making tentative approaches to the East Midlands; about this time a very deep boring of coal was made at Kingsthorpe, but without success, fortunately for the amenities of the village; while local subscribers were invited by an advertisement in the Mercury to contribute capital for the construction of "an intended railway from the Leicestershire colleries to the Leicestershire and Northamptonshire Union Canal. "This undertaking cannot fail to be a source of extensive and lasting benefit to the public, as well as advantageous to the subscriber".

What was the nature of the fields of service which presented itself to the congregational pioneers in St. James'? They found a cluster of cottages in the neighbourhood of the "Green Man" which, in its day, was a coaching hostelry of some note. In no sense could St. James' be regarded as a suburb of Northampton. Between its huddle of houses and the ruined castle walls which frowned down upon the Nasby branch of the Nene, lay a strip of waste or "moor", which was invariably flooded in winter. The narrow west bridge had an unsavoury reputation at night; if the Borough police ventured across it from Black Lion Hill. They faced the jeers and taunts of its inhabitants.

They were a rough, unruly crowd, to whom robbery and violence were commonplace, and of religious organisation there was nothing. Duston and Dallington, further afield, had their Parish Churches, and a Baptist Sunday School had been established at Duston in 1827.

The parent and focal point of congregationalism in Northampton was the famous "Castle Hill Meeting" and the name of Philip Doddridge is among the most honoured in the annals of the Borough of Northampton.

Mr. Bernards Godfreys extracts from the Castle Hill Sunday School account book for 1830.

What we are certain of is that in 1850 the St. James' Branch "was re-established in larger premises, the village smithy which stood at the junction of Mill Road and Main Road". A report given by Jonathan Robinson at the Castle Hill Church meeting of October 18th, 1858 tells us that "a small band of teachers laboured to instruct some fifty, sixty, or seventy scholars in a plain unadorned structure".

In St. James', something better was needed than the unattractive and inadequate quarters of the smithy, and the growth of the work led to the building of a School Room on the site known as "the piece", the new premises being opened on January 1st 1863. The following account is taken from the Northampton Mercury for January 3rd 1863.

"The completion of this neat, substantial, and commodious branch schoolroom, erected by the church and congregation at Doddridge Chapel, at a cost of £400, was celebrated on New Year's Day by a tea and after meeting. There were about a hundred children on the books, for whom the accommodation in the "blacksmith's shop", occupied for several years as a Schoolroom, was ill adapted.

Meanwhile, St. James's was increasing in population and changing in outlook; no longer was it the disreputable colony of outlaws of 1830, and the development of the factory system in our staple industry was shortly to determine its future prosperity. Another industry was the old foundry, which occupied the site of the present corporation bus depot, although a wide green belt still separated St. James's from the villages of Dallington and Old Duston, a number of new streets were set out, among which the school building occupied a very favourable position. It was liable to floods, which at times proved serious, but which were not without humorous elements. "It is on record that in the eighties, the ladies of the church were on one occasion cutting up in a side classroom for a tea party, when suddenly they saw water appearing on the floor and realised the dreaded floods had taken them unawares. Some were carried to safety, although one lady on the stout side had to be hoisted to the table, and we presume left there until the water had subsided," at least, she would not be short of provisions.

Still further accommodation was required in 1886, when new classrooms were added. At the half-yearly meeting held at Doddridge on September 30th Thomas Pressland reported on the special effort made by the poor of St. James's who raised £30 towards the alterations, beside paying the rent of the room at the cafe on St. James's Square, which has presumably required for a temporary classroom during the alterations. The progressive nature of the school is indicated by its mounting numbers. An old minute book has been preserved, which after recording the establishment of the "Sabbath School" in the new building in 1863, confines itself to band of hope reports. Such quotations as are given below appear exactly as in the original.

A subscription of one halfpenny a fortnight entitled the members of whom there were fifty six in the first half year, to a treat, to the rural seclusion of Dallington Park. After partaking of "the invigorating cup, with the usual accompaniments of cake, and bread and butter, to which they did ample justice. They enjoyed themselves by playing at blind buf, drop handkerchief, foot racing, hurdle racing, jumping etc., and some in high glee merrily toed the football."

The story of St. James's end is intimately associated with the firm of C.E. Lewis, which began in a modest way in Tanners Lane, Northampton in 1872. Larger premises were soon required – in Chalk Lane; the progressive shoe works in St. James's were erected in 1894. The founders of the business played a notable part in the nonconformist life of the district.

It was felt that the best expression of the sense entertained by congregational nonconformity in Northampton of Dr. Doddridge's life, character, and work and of the duty of congregationalists to do their share in supplying the need of a large and growing population, would be "a broad and generous scheme of congregational church expansion in the town". In St. James's end, "a Branch School and Preaching Station in connection with Doddridge Church had been established for some years, but the increase of the population and the demands of the work made a new Church imperative if Congregational Christianity was at all to keep pace with the pressing needs of the district. Here also an available site was at hand, and for the site and building £3,500 would be required. The stone-laying Ceremony at Doddridge Memorial took place on March 4th, 1896.

When the education league was established in St. James's in 1898 some of its more active workers were recruited from the two Nonconformist Chapels, Harlestone Road Primitive Methodist and Doddridge Memorial. At the time, St. James's had only the Church of England School – in common with the larger proportion of English villages, alternative teaching was provided at St. James's Hall – the Old Cafe on the Square, and the two Nonconformist Ministers, Rev. Jebez-Bell of Harlestone Road and Rev. T. Heale were responsible for arranging it. The controversy dragged on, some of its supporters "fell by the wayside," but the labours of the league bore fruit in 19 when the St. James's Council School was opened, with Arthur Sheard as headmaster, in a temporary building; affectionately called "the tin school", its temporary life was prolonged until the building of the Spencer Schools.

In 1903 the Church had the pleasure of counting the mayor of the Borough among its members, Edward Lewis having this honour conferred upon him; the same distinction befell his brother "T.D." in 1923.

Several members gained considerable distinction in the world of sport, such as Stafford Garnett and Fred Miller who played for Northampton Saints, outside-left for the Cobblers.

During Rev. T.F. Gilmore's ministry, the Sunday School Roll showed over 600 names. Rambles to Harlestone Firs provided a favourable halfday diversion for the teachers.

In 1910, to the regret of his many Northampton friends, Rev. T.F. Gilmore accepted a call to Gravesend. The years immediately preceding the War of 1914 were probably the most flourishing in the Church's History; Congregation was good, membership increased. In 1914 the Sunday School had some 700 Scholars and 60 teachers. The foundation stones were laid on November 29th, 1913 the year of the S.S. Jubilee Celebrations and temporary quarters were found for a very large body of children at Harlestone Road Central Halls. The Schoolbuildings, which cost £3,669, were opened on September 3rd, 1914 (which the troops occupying them just previously!) While the church extensions, including the new organ and the provision of substantial side galleries which increased the accommodation to 600, were completed shortly afterwards.

Frank Tomalin, senior, died in 1925, and for three generations to have played so conspicuous a part in the musical life of a Church is a remarkable record. His musical gifts have been inherited by his daughter.

Rev. J.R. McPhail's ministry concluding in 1922. Early in 1923 the new man was found in Rev. Bickley, B.D. Before the end of his first year at Northampton, Rev. H. Lewis following the precedent of his brother Edward in becoming the town's first citizen.

Edward Lewis, who had been part of the business world of the shoe trade for so many years, died in 1927.

Rev. W.C. Lazenby was Pastor of Castlecroft Congregational Church, Bury, until he received an invitation to succeed Rev. Harold Doddridge Memorial in 1935.

At the beginning of 1943, Rev. W.C. Lazenby removed to Wilmslow Congregational Church, Rev. P. Coxon, B.A., who like his predecessor is a product of Lancashire College, came to us in July 1943.

The Boy's Brigade
The idea of a company of the B.B. at Doddridge Memorial originated from a young Sergeant of the 1st (Doddridge) Company, which had been established in 1899, and which had attracted across the river a number of lads from St. James. In 1902 the idea became a reality, some twenty boys being temporarily officered by Lieutenants Harrison, Arnold Jeffrey and Brown of the 1st. On December 18th, 1902 the 4th (Doddridge Memorial) Company was formally enrolled, with Edward Lewis as Captain, and G.W. Whitford, M.E. Parkin, and Benjamin Thornton as Lieutenants.

A. Ll. Price was captain from 1904 to 1908, and James Heel from 1909 to 1921. During the first Great War thirty nine old boys gave their lives. In 1921 Albert Farey became Captain. Membership grew steadily, from twenty-three at its inception to about hundred in the middle thirties. The band established in 1921 with Mr. Ward as conductor, gave good musical service until 1939 War once more overshadowed the healthy activities of peacetime. The band was restarted, and had the honour of leading the civic procession on September 30th, 1946 with H.G. Lack, one of the original members in charge.

From the History of Doddridge Memorial Chapel E.F. Pool 1947.

1900

Doddridge Memorial Chapel showing Old Chapel Cottages.

1932. Doddridge Memorial Choir

Back row, left to right:
Wally Billingham, Mr. Oldham, Mr. Wiggins, Mr. Taylor, Mrs. Brown,
Mr. H. Lewis, Mrs. F. Howes, Mr. L. Thompson, Mrs. L. Chambers,
Mr. Stan Garnett, Mr. Staff Garnett, Mr. Billingham, Mr. E. Jones.

3rd row:
Mr. G. Knight, Mr. C. Harding, Miss N. Mitchell, Miss M. Brimley,
Miss E. Chambers, Miss J. Sanders, Mrs. B. Brown, Miss J. Brown, Miss G.
Thompson, Miss A. Coombes, Mrs. S. Garnett, Mrs. Aldous, Mr. J. Heel.

2nd row:
Mrs. E. James, Miss D. Starmer, Miss W. Mash, Miss E. Thorneycroft,
Miss E. Smith, Miss W. Brown, Miss M. Frost, Miss Woodland,
Miss F. Newman, Mrs. V. Billing, Miss N. Hobbs, Miss M. Tomalin,

1st Row:
Rev. W.C. Lazenby, Mr. M.E. Parkin, Mrs. C. Wills, Miss M. Mackness,
Miss V. Coombes, Miss M. Warren, Miss M. Billing, Miss O. Starmer,
Miss Billingham, Mrs. L. Chambers, Mr. F. Tomalin, Mr. A. Price.

1958

Doddridge Memorial Boys Brigade in St. James Road after Sunday morning parade, with Lieutenant Ron Harrison also Ian Poole, Terry Fisher, Mick Julian, Roger Broome, Tony Merry, Eddie Batchelor, Rodney Brown, David Yerell, Alan Burdett.

Harleston Road Methodist Chapel

The first Methodist chapel was built in Sandhill Road fronting on to the Weedon Road (then Duston Road). It all began in 1875 when James Watkins who later founded the Hopping Hill brick works came from Herefordshire, and being a strong Primitive Methodist, was chiefly responsible for gathering people together to build its first building to worship in. Meetings were held at the bottom of the six fields off Abbey Street and on the site of Victoria Park then part of Dallington Moors.

Mr. Watkins when he first came to Northampton was inspired by attending one of the early Primitive Chapels – Horsemarket, one can still trace these early Chapels by the foundation stones seen in the old Sandhill Road building, a reminder of faith and belonging in the early local chapels. Mr. Brimley a builder of St. James (later his son made high wooden circular vats for the leather tanning companies next to St. James Church), erected the Chapel for £345, in 1887.

Additions soon had to be made, a Schoolroom being built at the rear, and so well did the work prosper that both Chapel and Schoolroom were crowded, and it became necessary to find alternative accommodation. In 1892 the Cafe, St. James' Square, came on to the market, and a successful bid of £900 was made.
For the next seven years this was the home of St. James' End Primitive Methodist Church, but in December, 1897 an entry in a minute book says: "We recommend the Quarterly Meeting (the local Church Court of Methodism) to purchase a site for building a new Church and Schools at the corner of Sandhill Road and Harlestone Road".

Blocks of Duston stone from cottages which stood on the site (and which came in the first place from the ancient Abbey of St. James) were incorporated in the foundations. Costing £1,646, the Church opened for public worship in 1899.

At this time the Minister in charge was Rev. Jabez Bell, a forthright Lancastrian, who epitomises all that is implied in the term "The Nonconformist Conscience". This was evidenced in striking fashion in the late 1890's, when the religious life of St. James was in turmoil by reason of the controversy which raged between the Church of England (St. James' Parish Church) and Nonconformists. It became the "Great School War of 1899". Nonconformists fought for a "Board School" to prevent their children being taught Anglican doctrine in Scripture lessons, and the battle resulted in children of Nonconformist parents being withdrawn by invoking the Conscience Clause. For a time, Jabez Bell conducted his own Scripture lessons in his own "Church", the former Cafe.

The children concerned were given a medal to indicate that they were not to remain for Scripture teaching in the School. This led to more trouble, as if they refused to remove the medal they were barred from a whole morning's lessons. At a time when parents paid "School Money" each week for children's education, this further aggravated the situation. Feelings on both sides rose to such a pitch of unpleasantness that a public enquiry was held, resulting in the building of a "Board School" (the famous "Tin School") on the site of the present Corporation bus depot.

All this separation of Worship is thankfully a thing of the past and Meetings are held in Duston of all denominations not only for occasional combined worship but to discuss each Churches part in the future formation of worship and care towards the next 20,000 Northamptonians coming to live in this expanding area.

Harold Nash began his organists career at Harlestone Road before moving on to Park Avenue, his father was Choir Master for 27 years, followed by Bernard Harrison, Leslie Bodiley also served for many years as organist.

Today in a fine new modern building with up to date facilities for its members, Harlestone Road Methodist Church has moved a mile along the same road to be in the huge developing new areas of New Duston, they have a worship area seating 175, vestry, modern kitchens, classrooms, ample facilities for its growing youth organisations and a toilet, cloakroom block.

Alma Street

The older part built in 1878 has been pulled down as I have already mentioned, large families were brought up there. To rear them and feeding them was trial for the housewife, the husband usually striving at the boot factory to carve a wage from soul destroying piece work sought refuge in drink and backing horses, it was said that a bookmakers runner worked and took bets on every floor of one of the largest factories in St. James. I remember taking wreaths made at our shop in St. James, to various boot factories for the workers to see before it went on to the undertakers having lost one of their mates and they were all lip reading, so intense was the noise of continuous ground floor heavy machinery, powered by the overhead belts. Many a workman arrived home on a Friday night minus his full pay packet in old Alma Street due to drinking and betting.

One such man used to find his way home his wife told me after closing time, start to go up the stairs on his hands and knees counting the stairs one at a time, his problem was Devonshire Street was built the same time as Alma St. and he was so afraid he was in the wrong street his wife said when he got to the top of the stairs he would descend again then start again to make sure he had got the number of stairs right. This same man worked at the very top of the roof at the factory, mostly glass. He told me it was awful in Mid Summer he had to work all the harder to satisfy his thirst at the end of the day! Alma Street people were very helpful to one another. There was a very large strong woman who looked after births and deaths, the latter, I remember she would lay out the person in the coffin then the street would go in and pay their last respects, not many had black clothing suitable to attend the funeral. But all would follow and assemble outside every window in the street and curtains would be drawn. When an elderly person on their own was ill they were taken care of. I remember seeing neighbours putting an informed person in their bed right up against the front window, so they could help them if they needed attention. No front doors were ever locked except when we found a notice on the door such as diphtheria "Don't Enter".

Most families were clothed by the paying of so much a week after the money was left on the living room table, as most women had to go out charring of some sort. When King George Vth celebrated his 25 years on the throne, every table in the street came out end-to-end all the family chairs to sit down in two continuous lines to have tea together on this great occasion. It was one street one family of some 80 houses living together. We fished we caught the occasional rabbit for food, fishing was a necessary pastime but then needed the fish for the table. Some shoe workers would be up very early in the summer months collecting up their eel lines, put in the river overnight some walking a mile or more to sometimes to land a nice pike on the hook.

In 1920 there it was a boiling hot summer, water was short and there was an endless stream of people with prams and "Tate & Lyle" boxes on wheels going from St. James to Dallington to fetch water in tins, buckets, milk churns from a never failing watering once opposite Merthyr Road the rear of the old Dallington Hall Gardens. In a very hot summer, in these narrow streets like Alma St, privacy was limited. At night, the old Iron Bedsteads were pushed up to the open window for cool air. The movement of chamber pots on the bare boards could be heard. The yelling of the mother calling her large family off the streets as darkness approached, the one that came in late having a thrashing. The courting couple who kept every body awake after coming home after the pubs were shut taking too long to say goodnight and then a head would come out of an upstairs window and shout "Why don't you kiss her goodnight and go home", then a good swearing match would ensue in which all the heads would come out of the windows, Mrs. Norris at No. 6 supplied the needs of we children with her tiny sweet shop in which she supplied 1/2 penny gob stoppers 1/2 penny small cornet shaped bags filled with hundreds and thousands (very small sweets) tiger nuts and broken biscuits (taken from a sack). The football pitch was the street, from one manhole cover to the other, the flood lights, the street gas lamps. Did we run when a window crashed!

Hawkers shouting their wares galore, the fish man, Jimmy Ayres with his vegetables. The Knife Grinder Rag and Bone men all their hand carts etc. seem to be parked for long spells outside the "Forge Hammer".

1936

King George 5th Silver Jubilee Celebrations in Alma St. Group of residents who organised teas etc.

1936

Jubilee celebrations, Alma St. Some of the families from houses now demolished.

1936

Tea ladies on that memorable day.

The History of Upton (including Old Berrywood Hospital) is now being prepared for the next book.

F.G.